ATOMIC
FAITH

Praises for *Atomic Faith*

Atomic Faith has received enthusiastic praise from pastors, professionals, and everyday readers alike. These endorsements offer just a glimpse of the impact this book is having in the lives of those seeking to grow in practical, mountain-moving faith.

Featured Endorsements

John Burke, pastor / *New York Times* bestselling author, *Imagine Heaven*

In *Atomic Faith*, Dale eloquently guides us through Scripture—beautifully illustrated with captivating real-life stories—to reveal how active faith can accomplish great things. This book both inspires and challenges us to pray with bold confidence and expectancy that unleash God's power in our lives.

Randy Kay, bestselling author, *Heaven Stormed* and *Revelations From Heaven*

Wowza! *Atomic Faith* is a one-of-a-kind book that I believe will release God's miraculous power into the lives of readers. I love this book! Capt. Dale Black is one of the most devoted followers of Jesus Christ on the planet, and his insights reflect a spiritual maturity literally forged through the fire.

Nancy Sabato, podcast host, "The Call with Nancy Sabato"

This book is timely, inspiring, and the most impactful I've read on faith. In *Atomic Faith*, we meet people who faced life's toughest storms and chose to stand on God's Word.

Each chapter stirred my spirit and reminded me of the Holy Spirit's presence and power. Thank you, Dale, for showing how faith in action can lead to miracles.

Amy Peterson, PhD, counselor / women's ministry leader / retreat speaker
This powerful and compelling book on activating atomic faith is a must-read. Dale masterfully demonstrates how faith works, drawing the reader ever closer to God.

Pastor Steve Kang, founder, Revive the Nations and School of Ministers / church planter, SBC Send Network
What an amazing book! *Atomic Faith* shows that faith is a practical and powerful force. We learn that faith is often used as a verb—something that acts, endures, and believes in the goodness of a loving God. Through real-life stories of impossible obstacles and miraculous breakthroughs, Dale Black reveals how a life surrendered to God leads to answered prayers. As you read this book and apply its truths, you too can walk in overcoming faith!

Angelica Dunham, real estate agent
Wow. I'm learning how to make it happen. I'm now reading my Bible every day. *Atomic Faith* has changed my life!

Bob Joyce, pastor, Household of Faith – Benton, AR
Atomic Faith will strengthen your faith in God's Word and help you trust Jesus—even in the face of impossible odds. Capt. Dale Black's life is a true inspiration. Few testimonies have impacted me as deeply as his. The miraculous events

throughout his life and the global reach of his ministry are simply astounding.

Mike Guymon, captain, Boeing 787 Dreamliner
Atomic Faith is a powerful problem solver—which comes as no surprise. Everyone who knows Dale Black from the world of aviation and ministry sees his God-given gift for solving problems. Through faith, love, and divine intervention, Dale's story turned hardship into hope. In his best book yet, Dale shares the powerful, God-given principles he's learned through a remarkable life of faith and adventure.

Shawn Machen, pastor, World Victory Church – Moody, AL / author, *Unbelief: The Only Hindrance to Receiving from God*
Excellent book! Powerful. Simple. Life-changing. *Atomic Faith* is a must-read for every believer. It will deepen your understanding of the law of faith and challenge you to grow. Expect your faith to be strengthened and activated like never before.

David J. Giammona, US Army chaplain and colonel / president, Life Change / author, *The Military Guide to Armageddon*
Fantastic! A must-read. Dale Black is truly God's gift to mankind—and *Atomic Faith* is his gift to us. This powerful, uplifting, and authentic book delivers exactly what every believer needs in these end times.

Peggy Bean, childcare supervisor
This book gave me wisdom I didn't even realize I needed. It's taken my fear away—and replaced it with faith. Now, I finally understand what faith truly is.

Chris Henderson, radiologist
Atomic Faith is one of the best books I've ever read. I couldn't put it down once I started. I'm already gifting it to several friends.

Tim Tully, songwriter for television and movies / professional drummer / pilot, certified Part 107
Like Dale's other books, I couldn't put *Atomic Faith* down! It's packed with amazing real-world stories—featuring well-known and everyday people who overcame impossible odds through faith in God. It's easy to read and shows how God still performs miracles today, and with plenty of Bible references. It helped me understand the key differences between hope, belief, and faith. I loved every word of it!

Tim Breuninger, pastor, Foothills Christian Church Home Group
You'll love this book, which is filled with riveting stories—absolutely nothing dull! Dale is the real deal. He is a genuine, living Hall-of-Famer in God's Kingdom. Having read Dale's other books, I would have recommended *Atomic Faith* without even reading it first. But after reading the manuscript, I triple-recommend it!

Read more praises for Atomic Faith
at the end of the book.

Messages from Heaven Series

ATOMIC FAITH

Imagine Getting Your
Prayers Answered–
All of Them!

CAPT. DALE BLACK

BLACK EAGLE
PUBLISHING, LLC

ISBN: 978-1-965343-00-5 (Print)
ISBN: 978-1-965343-01-2 (E-book)
ISBN: 978-1-965343-02-9 (Audio)

Printed in the United States of America.

10 9 8 7 6 5 4 3 2 1

atomic

    1. The single irreducible particle of an element.[1]

    2. The source of immense constructive or destructive energy.[2]

faith

    1. Substance of things hoped for.[3]

    2. Evidence of things not seen.[4]

CONTENTS

INTRODUCTION

A LEGACY OF FAITH: MY FATHER'S GIFT AND CALLING

BY KARA BLACK (DAUGHTER)

SINCE MIRACULOUSLY SURVIVING WHAT WAS CLASSIFIED AS A "NON-SURVIVABLE" AIRPLANE CRASH, MY DAD, DALE BLACK, FULLY DEDICATED HIS LIFE TO GOD AND HIS CAREER TO AVIATION SAFETY.

After waking from a coma following the crash, he sensed a powerful transformation—his heart was filled with God's love. This newfound love compelled him to share the message of Jesus Christ with everyone he met.

Dad was in a wheelchair after suffering massive injuries in the accident. He faced a future that seemed impossible. But instead of giving in to despair, he turned to the Bible, searching for answers about faith. He needed more than just medical treatment—he needed miracles. To walk again, to see out of his right eye, to regain use of his arms, and to fly once more, he had to believe in something greater than what the doctors predicted.

Through studying Scripture, he discovered powerful truths about how faith works and began applying them to every part of his broken body. Against all odds and every medical prognosis, he did what seemed impossible. He walked again. His vision was restored. His memory returned and he regained full use of both arms. He became a living testimony to the power of God's Word—a walking miracle. In the end, he did more than just recover—he achieved his dream of becoming a professional airline pilot and later became an award-winning airline pilot instructor.

But the miracles didn't stop there.

Another compelling effect of the accident was the desire to improve aviation safety. For over fifty years, my dad applied his efforts, contributing his skills and experience toward training professional pilots and helping to prevent airplane accidents.

The Bible says, "A man's gift makes room for him, and brings him before great men" (Proverbs 18:16).

Dad believes he was given a gift from God that helped him uncover the causes of airplane crashes. He brought his gift into the airline pilot training company he started, where he strived to make pilots safer through his unique training programs.

Through his work in business and aviation, Dad played an essential role in the lives of celebrities, musical entertainers, and business CEOs. He trained many of them to fly various aircraft and built strong relationships as their instructor and aviation advisor. More importantly, he had the privilege of becoming friends with many of his clients, always sharing the love of God.

Dad was a flight instructor, pilot, or aircraft manager for John Travolta, Frank Sinatra, Merv Griffin, John Kennedy Jr., Karen Carpenter and husband Tom Burris, Captain and Tennille, James Brown, the Oak Ridge Boys, Bill Cosby, Dr. Bob Christiansen, Rich Buhler, Paul Crouch, Arthur Blessitt, Jake Steinfeld, Jacques Cousteau, Dr. Fredrick Price, Hal Lindsey, Jerry Savelle, Larry Ellison, Oral Roberts, Eric Thorson, Matthew Crouch, Dr. Julian Whitaker, Meadowlark Lemon, Alan Refkin, Shony Alex Braun, Jimmy Swaggart, Charlie Lyons, and Terry Fator. These were just some of his many high-profile clients—several of whom became his personal friends.

He also believed that God called him to pray for Elvis Presley, an ongoing practice that started in 1970 inside Elvis's JetStar at Long Beach Municipal Airport. (Incredible details in Chapter 20.)

Aviation also opened doors of friendship with leaders in the faith-based community, such as Demos Shakarian, Ann Kiemel Anderson, W. Shelburne Brown, Lorraine Day, MD, Jerald Johnson, Larry Garman, Tommy Barnett, Jack Hayford, Josh McDowell, Bill Burch, R. W. Shambach, Chuck Smith, Ralph Wilkerson, Tim LaHaye, and dozens more.

Important to understand is that although many of my dad's clients are listed here, this doesn't mean he agreed with their work, beliefs, or lifestyles. Dad saw himself as a missionary to each individual. He was ready to be used by the Lord Jesus however God chose.

He also never accepted payment for helping people in full-time ministry. On rare occasions when minister friends insisted on paying Dad, he would humbly accept and then quietly give 100 percent of the money back to their ministry.

Dad was invited to the White House by President Ronald Reagan and to the Knesset by Israel's Prime Minister Shimon Peres. Both are interesting stories. When President George Bush was in office, Dad was given a two-hour personal tour of *Air Force One* by the captain of the then-new Boeing 747 aircraft.

Through Dad's jet flight management and professional pilot training company, he met other politicians, business movers and shakers, professional football and baseball team owners, and film producers. Over time, he became a go-to guy for aviation in Hollywood, but Dad was never starstruck. He treated his celebrity clients with respect and integrity—but as equals, just like he did with everyone else. Dad's genuine love for Jesus spilled over to his clients, crediting him as the trustable man I know and love.

I've watched my dad share the love and message of Jesus across more than fifty countries. I grew up knowing that miracles weren't just stories—we lived them. In our family, God's Word was taken literally, and while that didn't mean we avoided hardships, it did mean we overcame them. Seeing firsthand how faith changes lives, both in my own family and around the world, has strengthened my trust in God and His promises.

Reading this book, you'll witness the miracles, stories, teachings, and principles that shaped my dad's heart, mind, and journey—and they have the power to transform your life too.

PART ONE

Faith in Action

Chapter 1

MY STORY

YOU MIGHT WONDER WHAT QUALIFIES ME TO TEACH ABOUT FAITH. My faith journey began at age nineteen when I was the sole survivor of a fatal plane crash. As a copilot in training, I built flight hours by flying cargo across California. My plans were on track, and my goals seemed within reach. In many ways, I was escaping a painful childhood, desperate to leave certain aspects of my personal life behind. Aviation was my way out, and I couldn't have been more motivated about my future.

The Crash

On July 18, 1969, disaster struck. Our Piper Navajo twin-engine plane crashed shortly after takeoff. The wing clipped the tops of several 110-foot trees, splintering them like kindling, which sent our aircraft head-on into a solid concrete and marble building at an impact speed of 135 mph. The National Transportation Safety Board deemed the crash "non-survivable."

The plane disintegrated into thousands of pieces, hurling the three pilots into a bone-crushing collision with the building, followed by a 100-foot free fall to the ground. Ironically, the building we crashed into was a mausoleum dedicated to deceased aviation pioneers, the Portal of the Folded Wings, which stands in the middle of the Valhalla Memorial Park Cemetery. Among those memorialized are famous pilots.

The crash left three pilots motionless at the scene, and witnesses assumed we were all dead.

Incredibly, I was resuscitated at the base of the crash site, where I was found compressed into what remained of the cockpit instrument panel. Clinging to life by a thread, I was rushed to a nearby hospital. My injuries were extensive and life-altering. Nearly every bone in my body was broken—both legs, knees, ankles, and arms were shattered, and my back was broken in multiple places. My right eye was nearly severed in half.

Blunt trauma had erased much of my memory, and my body was impaled with aircraft debris and chemically burned by fuel that soaked the crash site.

In the moments after impact, my spirit hovered above my body, observing the scene as a bystander. I suddenly realized I was a spirit with a soul who had lived in the broken body below. The overwhelming traumatic challenge of survival would ultimately define my future.

"I know the thoughts that I think toward you, says the Lord, thoughts of peace and not of evil, to give you a future and a hope" (Jeremiah 29:11).

Recovery

My recovery was slow and painful. But over time, the results were miraculous. As I sat in my wheelchair, with one functioning eye and only one usable arm, I did something for the first time in my life out of a desperate need for help. I immersed myself in the King James Version of the Bible, and God provided that help as I discovered His promises and instructions. I came to experience that God's Word is living and holds the power of life, healing, restoration, and blessing. Studying the Bible and applying its lessons became my lifeline.

My dream was to fly again. That feat required me to learn to walk again despite being told that I might never regain that ability. Likewise, I would have to learn to use my left arm, though I'd been informed that I would never be able to lift it.

As for my right eye, the diagnosis was equally grim. Experts said that if I were fortunate, I might become able to distinguish light from dark but would never see clearly out of that eye.

My goals of flying as a professional pilot were declared entirely out of reach—by everyone except me. The refrain I often heard whenever I expressed my hopes and dreams was, "You should be grateful just to be alive, Dale."

Of course, that was true, and I *was* grateful to be alive. But God had better words for me: *repentance, faith, surrender*, and words like *healing, restoration*, and *victory*. He taught me to trust Him and His Word and instructed me, "Walk by faith, not by sight" (2 Corinthians 5:7).

My greatest challenge was the naysayers. No one believed that my desires—nor what God had promised— were possible. Not my friends, parents, or doctors.

Yet God urged me to believe what He said about my situation and to agree with Him. Nothing I perceived with my physical senses and nothing I heard from the doctors gave me any hope of a normal body and life.

I would need a full box of new tools that would carry me toward becoming an overcomer.

While in that wheelchair, I discovered what the Bible teaches about hope, belief, and faith. As I studied Scripture, my relationship with Jesus grew into a partnership with God, which became the key to making the impossible possible. In this book, I share the story of my transformative journey and the life-changing lessons I learned about the miraculous power of faith.

> Jesus looked at them and said to them, "With men this is impossible, but with God all things are possible."
> — Matthew 19:26

Miraculous Faith

Little about my flying career could be considered legendary or historic. So I hope you'll forgive me if any part of this book sounds boastful, as that is not my heart or intention.

Although I later became a professional pilot, award-winning instructor, and aviation safety specialist, the challenging years of recovery taught me something even rarer. I discovered my true calling and reached my full potential—all thanks to focusing on developing and using faith in day-to-day living.

I believe the concepts in this book can help you do the same—regardless of your age, gender, or background. This book is designed to help you unlock your God-given potential and fulfill your purpose, just as I did and as many have who take faith actions on their beliefs.

By taking small steps of faith, your efforts will gradually compound into remarkable results. If you commit to these steps consistently, you'll find that anything is possible—because with God, nothing is impossible (Luke 1:37).

Everyone faces setbacks and challenges, but by incorporating small acts of faith into your daily life, you can overcome obstacles and achieve incredible outcomes.

Throughout my journey, I've encountered many successful individuals in business, government, Hollywood, and the entertainment industry—especially in music. None of them truly became overnight successes. Each worked diligently to refine their talents and gifts. And with the right support, they transformed small steps of progress into extraordinary achievements. They experienced results through human determination and actions. How much more can we accomplish with *God directing our steps* and empowering our outcomes?

Similarly, my journey wasn't defined by a single moment but by small victories and breakthroughs. I had to start with very modest beginnings and consistently build upon each success until I eventually achieved my goals. Considering the horrific crash and the extent of my injuries, my recovery was nothing short of miraculous.

Years ago, one of the successful authors I flew told me, "To write a great book, you must first become the book." At the time, I didn't fully grasp the wisdom in those words.

Looking back, I realize I was compelled to live out the principles I was placing my faith in. I didn't preach about faith from a pulpit; I lived it. I relied on small steps of faith to recover from multiple injuries and memory loss and to regain hope for living life after being resuscitated from death.

As I mentioned, one of my challenges was regaining vision in my injured eye. For over a year, I progressed from total blindness to perceiving light and dark, then to seeing fuzzy images, and finally to being able to read. Through prayer, perseverance, and declaring, "I walk by faith, not by sight," I eventually passed an FAA medical test with 20/20 vision in my injured eye—without glasses, Lasik, or contacts.

The incredible restoration of my vision lasted for the forty years of my professional career as a pilot. My excellent vision has continued by continuing my eye care routine. (To learn more about achieving better vision without glasses, see *Visiting Heaven*, Appendix A, page 287, available for purchase at daleblack.org.)

How This Book Can Benefit You

Since you're reading this book, you likely have unanswered prayers and still long for the answers. Possibly, you're sick and not sure how faith for healing works. Within these pages, you'll find the missing link to get your prayers answered.

We'll explore what faith is and how it works. I share step-by-step methods to increase your faith and experience remarkable results.

Everything I share in this book is grounded in the teachings of Jesus. The New Testament's *original text* supports all that I present. We will not use modern translations or paraphrases, as these have been changed and weakened in recent years.

By applying powerful biblical insights, unanswered prayer can become . . . a thing of the past.

Although Scripture supports what I've written, *Atomic Faith* is not academic or theological but intended for everyday people. Think of this book as an operations manual for your faith, interwoven with amazing stories of faith.

Across the forty years of my professional career, I've flown over sixty different aircraft types. Every plane I've flown had an operations manual written by experts and approved by the engineers who designed it. Manuals help pilots operate within the parameters of the aircraft's original design. Similarly, this book serves as an operations manual for exercising your faith—within the boundaries God designed.

No matter your background, age, gender, or current understanding of God, I believe *Atomic Faith* can help you experience consistent answers to your prayers, achieve healing, and bring about permanent life-changing results in your day-to-day life.

Just imagine getting your prayers answered—all of them.

Chapter 2

MIRACLE IN THE CANYON
THE DAVID ANDERSON STORY

"What man of you, having a hundred sheep,
if he loses one of them, does not leave the
ninety-nine in the wilderness, and go after
the one which is lost until he finds it?"
— Luke 15:4

A WELL-EXECUTED DEMONSTRATION IS ONE OF THE MOST POWERFUL TOOLS AN INSTRUCTOR PILOT CAN USE TO HELP NEW CAPTAINS TRUST THE TRAINING PROCESS, DEVELOP THEIR SKILLS EFFECTIVELY, AND GAIN CONFIDENCE. With that in mind, I've structured this chapter around a true story to illustrate faith in action. But this chapter is more than just a story—it demonstrates faith. I've included brief explanations of key faith principles to help you understand how faith works and how you can apply these principles in your own life.

The David Anderson Story

My wife, Paula, and I arrived at Uncle Jack's house in Long Beach to join our large extended family for a traditional Easter Sunday dinner. As Jack was about to pray over the meal, he asked the group to remember David Anderson and his family in our prayers. David had recently been reported missing and assumed lost in the Grand Canyon. He and his wife were members of the local church our family had attended for generations.

David had been hiking the canyon with the church group, and at the end of the day, he realized he'd left his jacket on the trail. "Go on ahead," he told the others. "I'll catch up."

Five days had passed, and David still had not been found despite the search party's efforts. Of course, there was great concern for his safety.

Though Paula and I knew David and his wife, Judy, as fellow attendees of the same church, we were only casual acquaintances. Yet as the Easter feasting began, neither of us could take a bite. My stomach churned in an irrational response to the news about David. Years earlier, I had learned not to dismiss the sensation but to recognize it as God stirring my spirit.

I turned to Paula and whispered, "Can you believe David is still missing?" Considering the urgency of his situation, I tried desperately to overrule my pounding heart (and God's nudging) with logic. *This isn't my responsibility. I barely know David and Judy.*

Tomorrow was Monday, and I was expected to lead the scheduled Jet-Type Rating class and conduct pilot training.

Flight students from several countries had already flown in for the class. My logical mind tried to manage what I was feeling. *I need to be present in the morning. How can I possibly leave? To even consider jumping into the middle of the search is unrealistic.* The spiritual and logical battle raged. *I don't have anything to do with this*, I rationalized.

Paula and I were both in turmoil, preventing us from enjoying the meal. We stepped into the backyard to talk. Before I could stop myself, I unexpectedly blurted out words that shocked me. "I really believe God is asking me to get involved in this."

At that very moment, a Scripture hit my spirit with great conviction, and I immediately shared it with Paula:

> "What man of you, having a hundred sheep, if he loses one of them, does not leave the ninety-nine in the wilderness, and go after the one which is lost until he finds it? And when he has found it, he lays it on his shoulders, rejoicing. And when he comes home, he calls together his friends and neighbors, saying to them, 'Rejoice with me, for I have found my sheep which was lost!'" — Luke 15:4–6

"Oh, Dale! That's the same Scripture that came to my mind!" she responded.

"Paula, look, we need to search for David until he's found. God has a plan to find him!" She nodded in agreement.

When God spoke to my heart that afternoon, it was an example of *rhéma*. In our English Bibles, the term "word" is translated from two different Greek terms: *rhēma* (which means spoken word) and *logos* (which means written Word). Throughout this book, these two terms will be used to help explain when and how God is speaking in a particular situation.

God's *rhēma* is a specific message or prompting we receive in the present, usually about a current situation or concern. The Holy Spirit speaks directly to the heart of a believer—Spirit to spirit. These messages are clear and often include Scripture.

When God speaks to your heart, His *rhēma* (spoken word) will always agree with His *logos* (written Word)—the Bible.

One of many Bible examples of God's *rhēma* is found in Luke 1:38, when a word from God was given to Mary. She responded, "Let it be to me according to your word" (*rhēma*), referring to the specific promise and message given to her through an angel.

When we act on God's *rhēma* word, His supernatural power is released into the situation. That action is an example of what I call *atomic faith*—faith powered by God that produces miracles. It's the kind of faith Jesus talked about in Mark 9:23: "All things are possible to him who believes."

Without hesitation, we made a plan. Paula would handle the company, using other available instructors in my absence, and I would start the seven-hour drive toward the canyon.

"Paula, why don't you call Judy and ask if she'd like to accompany me?"

We promptly excused ourselves from the family gathering. Time was of the essence.

As we reached our car, I grabbed Paula's hands and said, "Let's pray and believe right now that the Lord will direct us to His lost sheep and bring David home." We agreed in prayer: "God, please give us whatever we need to accomplish Your will. We will obey Your leading and search until we've found David—alive!"

Not even two hours had passed since learning about the ongoing crisis and search in the Grand Canyon, and I was already driving toward the destination with Judy. All the way, I focused on building her faith in God's promises. "Judy, when God says something, He does it. We must not doubt; we've got to both believe His promise with immovable faith. It's vitally important that we stay in agreement with God, no matter what circumstances we encounter. Can you do that?"

"I'll try," she said through tears, adding honestly, "It's just that I'm so afraid. Dale, it's already been *five days*."

Although stats were strongly against finding a missing person after five days, making David's chances of survival almost nil, I knew what God had spoken in me: *Search until he is found!* We had to be firmly determined to keep our faith intact, no matter what.

After driving for what seemed endless hours, we arrived at a canyon hotel late that night and checked into our rooms.

Early the next morning, I connected with Arizona Search and Rescue (SAR), the agency leading the search, and asked about their progress. The team leader, Steven, was a former Army reservist about my age. His team was former military plus a few civilian volunteers.

When I told Steven I was there to assist, his face quickly darkened. I couldn't imagine why. When I introduced him to Judy, his entire demeanor communicated that he didn't want anybody influencing his search plans and protocol. He told us in no uncertain terms that the best way to help was to leave him alone to accomplish his mission.

Before meeting Steven, I was told that approximately two hundred people had been looking for David on foot, but that number had dramatically dropped to only seventy. In addition, the SAR team had only one helicopter searching. Five full days had passed, and there was no trace of David.

Brian and Mark, loyal members of the church group, had refused to leave. Brian quickly filled me in with details of David's situation. "He was wearing tennis shoes, jeans, and a long-sleeved shirt. No hat or gloves. And whether he found his lightweight jacket remains unknown."

Although it was late spring, unforgiving snow still covered the ground—up to four feet in some places. Imagining what David must be experiencing was horrifying. Hypothermia was the most significant concern. Night temperatures were still dipping below freezing. SAR offered no ray of hope, informing us that survival in current conditions was unlikely after day three.

The unnerving yet undeniable statistics threatened to drain our faith. But I was determined to hold to the word I believed God had spoken in me. *Search until he is found!*

> When God speaks to your heart, satan arrives immediately to steal the word (Mark 4). How does he try to steal? He most commonly offers reports, stats, false teachings, opinions, etc., that provoke fear, doubt, and unbelief. In addition, he uses circumstances and people he can influence.

Early on day seven, I approached Steven. He was in the lobby near the SAR command center. "What time does your team start searching?" I asked.

His reply was a blow that angered me. "We're no longer looking for a living person; this is a recovery mission." Steven's attitude reflected a bureaucrat who didn't want to relinquish control and was locked into statistics.

We needed to quickly and drastically change our approach. My firm belief remained locked into God's *rhēma* message: "Search until he is found!" Our much different goals had reached an impasse.

Approaching the topic guardedly, I suggested, "What if we add another helicopter? Of course, we'll pay for it and all associated costs."

"No. No, no, no!" Steven barked like an indignant child. Apparently, the suggestion felt threatening to his need to be the leader. "We can't have two helicopters in the same airspace. It's just too dangerous—"

"Wait just a moment," I cut in. "I'm an airline pilot, ATP instructor, and FAA jet examiner. I own a jet charter company, so I know a little about aviation. Surely our odds of finding David will improve with more eyes searching."

"No way, Dale!" he snapped. "That's not going to happen!"

As he turned on his heel, I insisted, "Look, I'm working on behalf of God and as a volunteer, assisting that woman, David's wife." I pointed toward Judy. "You're working for the state of Arizona. Your assignment is to search and rescue. Why don't you search according to your rules, and I'll search according to mine." It wasn't a question; I was no longer asking. "I can search where you're not. Let's at least work in agreement with each other."

> Expect resistance. Satan always offers what seems like logical reasons to let go of your faith. However, if God has spoken in you, that word must be protected; God expects you to hold firm in true faith.
>
> He has given us superior power and weapons to go toe to toe with satan and his agents. Learning to use those spiritual tools and remaining equipped and practiced for whatever arises against God's Word (*rhēma* and *logos*) is paramount to accomplishing the mission of faith. (Read Ephesians 6 and James 4:7.)

Obedience to God overruled Steven's resistance, and I pursued a private chopper.

I asked Paula to charter a helicopter and pilot, and I specified our needs, emphasizing my request for a Jet Ranger. Despite the extra expense, I knew we would contend with strong winds in and around the canyon. For safety, the chopper needed to be jet-powered.

Paula and I had a small amount of reserved funds in savings, and we decided to use those for the helicopter. We needed more eyes in the air—and fast!

Within two hours, the helicopter reached the canyon. Bill, the pilot, was young and eager. He and I were instantly in sync. Providentially, as our helicopter arrived, the SAR chopper was grounded. Word was that it had broken down, and they were waiting for a new part that would take at least three days to arrive.

I still believe the helicopter hadn't actually broken down. I think Steven, feeling personally threatened, had refused to cooperate and fabricated the story about a mechanical issue—willing to let a man die because of his pride and need for control.

Brian, who had been part of the search from the very beginning, quickly learned how to read aviation maps with my guidance. We stayed in direct contact using handheld radios, and I coordinated everything from the ground. I informed Bill, "Fly wherever Brian instructs if safe to do so. Remember, *search until he's found!*"

My expedient role was to work from the hotel to coordinate our ground and flight search teams and stay in direct communication. We were using the aviation radios I'd newly purchased for this mission.

While we searched by air and ground, the park rangers continued traversing the trails, looking for clues. They were good at what they were trained to do, and we learned a lot from their experience.

In years prior, I had hiked the Grand Canyon a dozen times and piloted scenic tours over the massive grandeur of the Rocky Mountains and her deep, winding gullies. I was familiar with her complexities and threats. During summer, daytime temperatures commonly reach 90 degrees, even up to 120.

In such extreme conditions, a hiker without enough water and shade can quickly become dehydrated and disoriented. In the other seasons, the frigid nights threaten hypothermia to the unprepared or lost hiker. Such extreme conditions cause illnesses that can lead to death. As hikers become hypothermic, their bodies grow dangerously cold, but they feel hot. This phenomenon can cause them to shed their clothing. Those who die in such circumstances are often found naked or nearly so.

The search was taking place in April. Winter snow was still on the ground, and nighttime temperatures dropped well below freezing. But our small team's big faith in God and His promise kept us going. We agreed that no one would speak about statistics or finding a deceased David. Atomic faith was needed if we were to witness the miraculous.

Still, a fight is a fight, which the Bible talks about as "the good fight of faith" (1 Timothy 6:12). I encouraged our team, "We'll search *until he is found*—alive—according to God's *rhēma* and our prayers and faith!"

Three people were in the chopper. As Bill flew the Jet Ranger, Brian and Mark each searched from their respective sides through binoculars, looking for any signs of David. The long-range radios maximized our efforts with quality communication.

Our entire team was feeling the pressure of time. In daylight hours, no one rested or even stopped to eat. We knew that every hour mattered.

I stood on the rim, about 6,000 feet above the canyon floor, watching the chopper and ground searchers as they gradually disappeared. How anyone on a trail could become disoriented and lost was easy to understand. The main canyon branched into smaller canyons, weaving a maze of pathways that were easy to follow, but many trailed to dead ends. Perspective from the canyon floor was impossible— the gorge was too massive at 1.2 million acres, 277 miles long. Finding a lost person was like looking for a needle in a haystack.

I whispered another prayer of conviction. "Heavenly Father, thank You for hearing me and for answering prayer. Thank You for bringing David back alive."

The sheer scale of the canyon soon swallowed the helicopter as though it were a gnat. I reflected again on the Scripture Jesus taught and I chose to believe: The shepherd will leave the ninety-nine to search for the one lost sheep— search until he's found and carry him back with joy!

On that Easter Sunday, just two days prior, Paula and I knew we had to respond to God's direction by becoming His hands and feet: *taking action* as a way to live out our atomic faith.

We were now at the passing of the seventh day since David had disappeared and without so much as a trace since. Unfortunately, discouragement was setting in. *How can this be happening?* My disappointment was difficult to hide. Concern was grooved into everyone's faces.

Most volunteers had left, reducing our group to a mere four. Although we still had the helicopter, we felt gutted. The lack of ground searchers would limit our efforts to the air. Complicating the dire circumstances were the dwindling funds, dictating we had only one more day of flying.

Adding to our growing frustration, SAR decided to wind down their search. Their supposedly grounded helicopter and the near-zero statistical chance of finding David alive had prompted them to pack up.

By the morning of the eighth day, we were entirely alone—the four of us. The assault on our faith was ferocious. At that point, holding onto faith that we would find David, much less alive, was humanly illogical. Even ridiculous.

My thoughts traveled to Jesus's disciples. They'd had similar thoughts as they faced the impossibility of feeding exponentially more than five thousand people with only five loaves and two fish on hand.

As I wrestled with what to do, God gently spoke His Word from ages past to my heart, the declaration and plea by His prophet Moses to God's people:

> "This day I call the heavens and the earth as witnesses against you that I have set before you life and death, blessings and curses. Now choose life, so that you and your children may live." — Deuteronomy 30:19

Since the beginning of time, faith has been a matter of one's *choice*.

Once again, I had to choose between acting in faith (staying and searching) or reacting in doubt (returning home) based on circumstances and statistics. Each member of our four-man team had to choose.

Faith is acting on what you believe.

Faith begins with hope and grows into belief. That belief becomes stronger when you're convinced that what God says is true. When that belief takes root in your heart, faith can show itself through your actions.

Even when the answer isn't visible in the natural world, atomic faith takes action based on your belief in God's living, supernatural Word. At first, the answer may only be seen in your heart, but your faith-filled actions build the substance of faith in the spiritual realm. In time, your faith brings the visible answer you've been believing for.

Because atomic faith is essential, I'll say this again: Faith is acting on what you believe.

Using a chart and the knowledge I'd gained from those who had previously searched the ground and from the air, I guided Bill into an airborne search grid over a yet-unscoured area.

At every radio crackle, I grabbed the receiver in anticipation. *Is this it? Has David been found?*

Again, the hours ticked by as the team searched, finding nothing—not a hint—and sunset was approaching. The fading sky seemed to mock us and threaten to bury us in the darkness of doubt and hopelessness.

There was a crescendo of tense apprehension among us as dusk slipped further into blackness with no sign of David as if he had vanished into thin air. But we knew that God knew exactly where David was.

I radioed Bill. They had landed the chopper on the rocky rim, needing further instruction. I carefully considered how much search time remained. Like the fading daylight, the fuel was low, and funds were nearly gone. *Maybe an hour tomorrow, two at the most.*

Logically, this search was over. Spiritually, we tightened our grip. *This is warfare!* Spiritual warfare required "*above all,* taking the shield of faith with which you will be able to quench all the fiery darts of the wicked one" (Ephesians 6:16, author emphasis). "Above all," we needed to hold tightly to faith and stand firm.

Scripture held me up: "Having done all, to stand. Stand therefore" (Ephesians 6:13–14).

We had done everything possible to stand against the Grand Canyon of defeat. Now, "above all," we needed to continue standing against the enemy's threats—no matter what.

Bowing my head, I prayed aloud, "Lord? Lord? What shall I do now, Father?" Everything was on the line.

Due to the resistance that faith encounters, *perseverance* is always required. Perseverance (endurance) was another essential element of obeying God's directive—"Search until he is found"—and receiving His promise.

> If we hope for what we do not see, we eagerly wait for it with perseverance. — Romans 8:25

The chopper and its weary crew rested in the cold silence on the rim of the vast, dark canyon as I prayed in the hotel lobby. Again, I sensed God's familiar, quiet voice in my heart, this time from Luke 15:4, Jesus speaking:

> "What man of you, having a hundred sheep, if he loses one of them, does not leave the ninety-nine in the wilderness, and go after the one which is lost *until he finds it?*" (author emphasis)

Through the radio transmitter, I asked the three men, "Would you be willing to stay there overnight and search in the morning for a couple of hours?"

My request surprised them. The night temperatures were freezing, and there was nowhere to lie down. If they agreed to stay, they would have to huddle in the helicopter for warmth and wait nine hours for sunrise. *If I can compel them to stay until morning, we'll have a final two hours with the helicopter to search.*

An early morning search would also provide longer shadows, adding visual help to see a lost hiker.

If the guys decided to fly back to the motel tonight—which most people would have—that would end our search. But if they were willing to sacrifice comfort by spending the night in the helicopter, that would give us an additional, precious two hours.

But the search had stretched all of us to what seemed our limit. We were each waging an inner war of faith against logic, statistics, emotions, physical comfort, and much more.

Pilot Bill called his boss and got approval to stay another day, forfeiting his day's salary. Then the other two men agreed to stay.

I was on the ready too. The radio was close by my side as I lay on the hotel lobby floor.

At about 5:30 a.m., the radio crackled. "Dale? We're ready to fly." I led the team in prayer. "Father, in the name of Jesus, we thank You for hearing our prayer. Lord, lead us to David. Direct us to find him alive. Thank You, Jesus. You always answer prayer."

Faith, I'd learned, is always easiest to give up in the eleventh hour, when hopelessness stirs and grows. From our human view, time had run out. I struggled to keep my mouth from speaking what was evident: *We're out of time and options!*

This flight was, in fact, the final return to base operation.

This time, we would take a strategically different route.

I gave final instructions. "Brian, fly the route we agreed on—unless you're sure God is leading you elsewhere."

The helicopter headed south, low on fuel. Silently and desperately, Brian and Mark combed the landscape with binoculars.

Suddenly, Brian broke the silence with an exhilarated yell. "There! I see something!"

Bill turned the helicopter slightly so they could all see below. Strewn along the snow was a trail of clothing—a jacket, shirt, socks, and shoes—the telltale signs of a hiker who'd discarded clothes in the final stages of hypothermia.

The radio crackled again. "Dale! We see a nearly naked man on a rock below. It's got to be David! We think we've found him!"

I was startled and stunned. A surge of emotions collided in me—overwhelming shock, profound relief, and a landslide of gratitude struck hard against my concern for David's well-being.

Is he alive? He has to be alive! Are we too late? God is never too late!

Near breathless, I waited, heart pounding, praying in praise, wonder, joy, excitement, and concern.

The team reported that the man had attempted to stand on a large rock and then collapsed into a heap. They watched in disbelief and anguish as he fell off into the snow. I would later learn that David had mustered what little strength he had to stand again, having heard the chopper overhead and hoping to be seen.

The man has to be David! He was a tall man who had always been slim. The man below matched the description, though he was a bag of bones. Despite all odds, he was alive! But barely. He had been suffering in subfreezing temperatures for over a week, with no access to food or water and wearing little clothing. He was too weak to get back up. He lay lifeless in the snow.

The helicopter landed, and Brian and Mark ran to the collapsed man. They hastily wrapped him in a blanket and carried him to the helicopter.

The radio crackled. "Dale! We've got him! Dale! It's David! He's alive!"

"I copy! I copy! Praise the Good Lord! He's alive!" I shouted.

With wonder, I whispered God's words: "Until he's found." Then, with great, surging emotion, "Thank You, Father! Thank You!"

Suddenly, Judy appeared, running into the lobby, screaming, her face wet with tears. "What's happening?" she cried. "What's happening?"

I grabbed her by each arm. "They found him, Judy! He's alive! Praise God! He's alive!"

We barely breathed as we waited for the chopper to touch down.

David was barely recognizable. He was about six feet four inches, yet as I lifted his frail, diminished body into my arms, he couldn't have weighed more than a hundred pounds. Judy gasped and flung her arms around him, heaving sobs of relief, joy, concern, and wonder.

God was faithful to His promise in response to our obedience and stalwart faith. In faith, we had stood with perseverance and stayed the course, agreeing with God's directives and the promises of His Word. Our atomic faith had linked His power and will to Earth as it is in Heaven.

Through the immense challenges—all that the enemy had thrown at us to steal our faith—we chose to remain determined and faithful to God's instruction and promise. We had stood firmly, believing our Father even when human doubt seeped in. We had fought the "good fight of faith" to a victorious end: David was found alive; God's promise was fulfilled.

"The eyes of the Lord run to and fro throughout the whole earth, to show Himself strong on behalf of those whose heart is loyal to Him."
— 2 Chronicles 16:9

The next day, we received news that David's internal organs were shutting down before his rescue. The doctor stated the obvious: "David's body was in the final stages of hypothermia. Death was only hours away."

A week or so later, I was working at my desk when Paula walked in. She was wearing a huge smile and carrying a large, beautiful bouquet. Teary-eyed, she read the accompanying note.

> Dear Dale, you saved my life! I am forever in debt to you.
> May God bless you and Paula always!
> — David Anderson

> Thank you, Dale, for never giving up! *Until he is found!!!!* — Judy

The Takeaway
Credit for David's survival goes to God, His Holy Spirit, and His living Word. Also, to our small rescue team: Brian, Mark, Bill, and, of course, Paula and me. Yes, God's still,

small voice had prompted me to join the search for David, but my wife and I had choices wrapped in hard questions:

- Will we believe the inner prompting and message is God's voice?
- Does the message align with His written Word?
- Will we put everything else aside and act on what we believe is His voice and instructions?
- Will we stand firm with atomic faith and not give in to doubt and hopelessness, no matter what? *No matter what?*
- Will God come through?

We each chose to believe.

 We each chose to obey and take action in faith.

  We each chose to agree with God's *rhēma* and *logos* (words).

   We each chose to stay in the battle and fight the good fight of faith, no matter what, even when it came down to only four remaining searchers.

    We each chose to persevere, more so when the possible looked utterly impossible.

    We each chose atomic faith.

And God faithfully fulfilled His promise.

> Show me your faith without your works, and I will show you my faith by my works. — James 2:18

Once our team had prayed in faith, we were to believe God's promise as *having already taken place in Heaven.* From that moment forward, our responsibility was to act in atomic faith as though the answer was *already in our hands.*

As difficult as the search was, we had fought the good fight with atomic faith. Spiritual warfare had been enormously challenging; the enemy always ensues when we follow God by faith. But the power of the Holy Spirit with our unwavering faith enabled us to continue standing and believing.

Even when our faith had dwindled to the size of a mustard seed, we each determined to remain standing in faith—a choice, a mindset of atomic faith for what we were choosing to believe: David will be found—and found alive.

Against satan's fiery darts of lies, doubts, and mockery to our hearts, we had chosen to remain unyielding and hold tighter to the shield of faith.

Faith is more than hope.
Faith is different from believing.
Faith is acting on what you believe.

The story of Gideon's army—reduced from 32,000 to 300 men—parallels our search for David in the Grand Canyon. We had started with 205 searchers, but only 4 remained by the final days.

The test of our faith was a powerful reminder that God calls us to trust Him when circumstances seem impossible. The outcome underscores that *faith*—not resources, science, or logic—is the key to answered prayer.

PART TWO

What Is Faith?

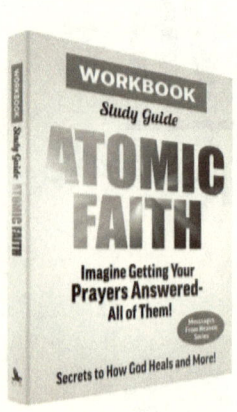

Chapter 3

WALKING BY FAITH
THE STORY OF PUTTING
FIRST THINGS FIRST

Without faith it is impossible to please
Him, for he who comes to God must believe
that He is, and that He is the rewarder
of those who diligently seek Him.
— Hebrews 11:6

UNDERSTANDING HOW FAITH WORKS CHANGES EVERYTHING. I'm living proof of this and fully convinced that faith is *the* most important aspect of living as Jesus taught His followers to live.

Are you seeing miracles in your life?

Are your prayers being answered?

Are you overcoming the obstacles you face?

If your answer is *no* or *not often,* this book is for you.

What is faith, and how does it work? *Atomic Faith* answers those questions and more—and might just be the treasure chest you've been searching for! This book is likely to be the missing link to getting your prayers answered and the tool to uncover the secrets of how God heals. And so much more.

Without faith, can prayers ever get answered?

Without faith, how does anyone overcome evil or view adverse circumstances as blessings?

Without faith, how do miracles occur?

Getting the answers we need when we pray is impossible without faith. And without faith, accomplishing God's will is not possible.

Faith is the currency of Heaven, just as the dollar bill is the currency of the United States.

But what does *faith* really mean?

I've experienced that people are often confused about the definition of *faith*, thinking it means what they *believe*. For example, we hear and ask this common question, "What faith are you?"—causing us to think that faith is about our religious beliefs and practices.

Interestingly, the Bible presents the term *faith* as both a noun *and* a verb. We occasionally see *faith* used as a noun, like the above example. But most often throughout the Bible, we see *faith* used as a verb—an action word. Jesus certainly used it that way.

My hope is that through this book, your understanding of faith as an *action* will be your big *aha* takeaway, which could be life-changing.

Understanding faith as an action means that God's awesome power is always available to you in daily life.

When we use faith as a verb, an incredible spiritual channel opens that causes the power of God (the greatest force imaginable) to move from Heaven to Earth. *That* is what will change your life.

Using faith as a verb causes the power of God to move from Heaven to Earth.

Faith used correctly requires putting first things first. To help you understand how atomic faith works, I've included an example of faith in action as a verb.

The Story of Putting First Things First

After surviving the plane crash, one of my biggest physical challenges was my left ankle. It had been badly damaged in the 135-mph crash into the building, followed by a ten-story fall. Doctors were sure I'd never walk again. With another major surgery, I might be able to put weight on it standing, but my leg would be much shorter, and my ankle was stiff and immobile. Becoming an airline pilot seemed impossible.

Dr. Graham (acclaimed for being Evel Knievel's doctor) again recommended I have bone-fusion surgery and accept the downside. "The blood flow through the bone is nonexistent, Dale. If it doesn't improve, the bone will die and collapse."

Immediately, my thoughts turned to faith, and I reminded myself of Hebrews 11:1: "Faith is the substance of things hoped for, the evidence of things not seen."

"Evidence"—as with the hard facts lawyers present that must stand up in a court of law. I was beginning to understand how faith works.

Before the crash, I wasn't familiar with faith. Now I needed it for almost everything. However, due to my inexperience with faith, I had not considered the negative impact of discouraging words, disappointing circumstances, and devastating medical reports.

My first unexpected detour came when my father heard I had decided not to have the surgery. "Dale, I think you're being foolish," he stated.

All I could think about was how the surgery would permanently banish my dream of becoming an airline pilot—and that was not okay with me.

"No, Dad," I responded with determination. "I've made up my mind. I've asked God to heal my ankle."

When friends would ask how I was doing, I gave my standard reply, speaking in faith according to what I believed. "God has healed me. Soon, I'll have new X-rays to prove it!"

When it was time for my next doctor's appointment, I gathered five friends who wanted to see a miracle firsthand. We piled into a friend's old green Cadillac and headed to Burbank.

Walking into Dr. Graham's office, I pointed to my friends and boldly said to him, "They're here to see a miracle—God has healed my ankle."

X-rays were taken, and we waited anxiously while Dr. Graham placed the negatives on the screen. He paused for what felt like forever. Finally, he spoke. "There's absolutely no progress, Dale. I'm sorry. The blood is not circulating in your ankle."

Shock went through me like lightning. Even though the war was far from over, that small battle felt like a huge loss. *What went wrong?*

Deep down was a surge of embarrassing thoughts. I realized I had slipped back into self-centeredness. Frustration boiled up in me, fueled by those tidy, oversimplified answers and clichés about healing. *My life is on the line!* Doubt directed me to the unsettling possibility that maybe Dr. Graham was right. Maybe my decision to trust God for healing had consequences far worse than I was willing to admit.

Having confidently told hundreds of people that my ankle was healed, I was now reeling between doubt and faith. All because the X-rays showed no improvement.

The realization that I had put more trust in the medical report than God's promise embarrassed me. I had let myself believe more in the circumstances—the diagnosis—than in the truth of God's Word. *How could I have allowed that to happen?*

Determined to persevere through this spiritual test, I again immersed myself in the Bible, replacing my doubts with belief in God's promises.

Days later, I shared at the college chapel service how my faith for healing had been tested. And I explained how God's Word had strengthened my belief in His promises for answered prayer.

With strengthened faith, I again invited several friends to join me for my next appointment with Dr. Graham. I was confident we would witness a miracle this time.

The previous appointment had been a test of my faith, and I had failed miserably. Much later, I learned that God doesn't waste even our failures. It's often in failure that we learn and grow.

I now understood where I'd gone wrong. I'd been living with the mindset that *seeing* is believing. But faith operates differently. The Bible teaches that believing leads to seeing.

> Faith also requires resistance. Bringing Heaven's answers into a fallen world stirs opposition. Satan works relentlessly to steal faith, using challenges, negative reports, and troubling symptoms to plant fear and doubt. His tactics are to foster unbelief, the very opposite of faith.
>
> Now faith is the substance of things hoped for, the evidence of things not seen. – Hebrews 11:1

Two weeks later, my friends and I arrived again at Dr. Graham's office, anxiously gathered at the viewing screen in anticipation of what the new X-rays would show.

I briefly explained to Dr. Graham that I had previously misunderstood the workings of faith. "I had been distracted by the circumstances instead of keeping my focus on God's promises." We joined hands to pray, and I thanked God for the truth of His Word and His power to heal.

Dr. Graham placed the X-rays on the screen, and I concluded that his patience was thin. Finally, he turned to me, his expression frustrated and heavy. "Dale, I'm sorry," he began, clearly grappling with the words. "Not only has there been no improvement, but now we've waited too long." A quake of disbelief hit me. "There's no blood circulation in your ankle," he explained, "and there's nothing we can do to reverse this. The bone is completely dead."

I was stunned. *How can this be happening?* I had corrected my previous errors. Yet the outcome was diametrically opposite of what I'd expected. My heart was crushed by the weight of his declaration of doom, and my mind was a fierce storm of questions. *If I can't trust God, who or what can I ever trust again?*

The news had rendered me speechless.

We drove back to campus in silence, the tension palpable. I didn't want to talk to anyone. I felt foolish and embarrassed.

I hurried to my room as fast as my crutches would allow, shut the door, and locked it. Overwhelmed by the flood of doubts and fear, I collapsed in despair.

You're a fool, Dale Black, I berated myself—*a complete idiot for trusting God so fully with so much at stake. You clearly don't know what you're doing. And now you'll never walk again!*

Grief for my lost future, hopes, and ambitions consumed me. *Forget about sports and flying. Those dreams are gone forever,* I lamented in anger. *All because of your foolish faith experiment! God doesn't heal everyone!*

Bitter human reasoning had risen and taken control. *You can't just decide God will heal you and then expect to be healed, Dale! You made a huge mistake by not going through with the surgery. You might have at least walked again. But no,* I jeered, *you had to act like some big man of faith.*

With every new, crushing thought, my spirit sank deeper into an abyss of nothingness. *How could you have been so stupid? Now you've lost everything!*

Sitting or lying down was uncomfortable due to my various casts and braces, so I was on the floor beside my bed in the least painful position: on my knees. I would later see that this practical position had become my spiritual posture before God. I was at my lowest in every regard, kneeling, alone, and choking on desperation.

I didn't want to see anyone. I only wanted to deal with God—and my thoughts and words weren't particularly reverent. "God, You've messed up!" I exploded. "I've made a fool of myself in front of the medical staff and my friends. Now my life is ruined! And this situation has also damaged *Your* reputation!" I added angrily. "Worst of all, my career goals are dead! *And* I'm crippled for life!"

Though I knew I was entirely wrong in blaming God and raging at Him, I'm ashamed to admit that my rant continued. I fired a round of questions at Him. "Why didn't You keep the promises You made in the Bible? I thought I could trust You!" I shook my head in disbelief. "Are You playing some kind of game with me?" I paused as though expecting a response.

Then my thoughts took a different direction. "I did everything—*everything*—I was supposed to!"

Didn't I?

A faint cloud of doubt hovered. Still, I charged Him with another round of blame. "But You didn't hold up Your end of the deal. Can You explain why?" I demanded, falling deeper into the bottomless void. "What more do You want from me, God? Do You *really* want me in a wheelchair for the rest of my life? Well, congratulations!" I jeered. "That's exactly what You got!"

I dropped my forehead onto the edge of the mattress. I was spent—exhausted physically, mentally, and emotionally by the circumstances and my broiling outbursts. I felt as though robbers had invaded me, stolen everything, beaten me, and left me for dead. I was a shell of the man I had been a mere hour before, now empty, lost, and alone.

There were no more tears; they had run their course. My sobbing was over, like my hopes and dreams.

"Dale," a clear yet gentle voice spoke to my heart. "Why do you want to be healed so badly? Seek first My kingdom and My righteousness, and all these things will be added to you."

Startled, I momentarily forgot my self-centered thoughts and immediately remembered reading that Scripture several times recently from Matthew 6:33. But somehow, I had glossed over "His righteousness." God's voice in me had touched a deep valve, and tears once more trickled down my cheeks, fogging my one good eye.

Again I heard His voice. "Seek Me first, Dale. And My righteousness," He pressed. "And all these things will be added to you."

I knew exactly what He meant and now what I had missed during my weeks of determined faith. I had not put first things first in my journey of faith. I had been more focused on the healing than on the Healer. I had wanted a miracle more than the Miracle Maker.

"His righteousness" echoed in my mind and pounded on my heart. *His righteousness. His righteousness. . . .*

Despite my best efforts, I recognized that my heart and life were not entirely pure. A light had reached into the shadowed crevices, revealing lingering sins I had been reluctant to confront. My stubborn insistence on a miracle had crawled to the forefront in full view.

Although I had genuinely believed that my prayers were intended to glorify God, it became clear that I had been more focused on the blessings I hoped to receive than on the God who provides them.

In that pivotal moment, everything in my heart and mind shifted to a new spiritual posture. I was ready to fully surrender my all to God—my desires, hopes, and, more importantly, my thinking, will, feelings, and my now-well-lit sins.

"God, I give You every corner of my life and every measure of control. They're Yours. I'm Yours—mere clay in Your hands to reshape for Your glory.

"I'm so sorry, Lord. I know that every day is a gift from You. What's clear to everyone, especially me, is that Dale Black should have died in that plane crash. I have nothing left to lose. Whether in a wheelchair or not, I'll serve You."

The stillness and peace of surrender invited more thoughts and questions of reflection, no longer fueled by anger and despair. They were now calm ripples in a glassy, reflective sea.

Again I fell before the Lord and wept. I relinquished my obsession with walking again, my dreams of flying and playing sports, and my pursuit of gaining respect from others. I surrendered everything—all of me and all the moments to come. "Lord, it's all in Your hands now. I give You full control of my life. However, . . . I'm still convinced by Your Word that healing is Your will. So I'm going to continue praying for complete healing."

I reminded Him what Jesus had said from Mark 1:24: "Whatever things you ask when you pray, believe that you receive them, and you will have them." I quickly added, "But this time, I'll put *You first* in my life."

Then and there, I had decided that no matter the cost, I would serve God with my whole heart, soul, mind, and strength. I'd let go of my selfish goals and plans, giving everything to Him. Then I said something I would never have imagined saying. "God, if You can use me better in a wheelchair, as a cripple, then not my will, but Yours be done."

I truly meant every word. I had honestly and completely surrendered my all to Jesus.

At that moment, I experienced something extraordinary: a physical sensation, as if a warm, rich substance akin to oil pouring over my head and cascading over every part of me. The feeling was overwhelming and unforgettable.

Filled with joy and peace, I felt utterly free.

A few days later, I spoke again at the Wednesday night chapel service. I shared a simple message about submitting ourselves to God in every area of life, and I didn't mention my ankle. My conversations had shifted from talking about external miracles to the importance of a broken self-will and surrendered heart to Jesus that places Him as Lord over our lives.

When the time came for my next appointment with Dr. Graham, I arrived alone. I hadn't invited anyone to come along.

Two weeks had passed since I'd surrendered my all to Jesus and experienced the warm, oil-like covering, and two weeks since I'd resigned myself to a life in a wheelchair, should that be God's will.

On the way to Dr. Graham's office, I made a detour to Valhalla Memorial Park, the site of the airplane crash. I paused at the Portal of the Folded Wings, the mausoleum we had crashed into. The site had become my place for reflection since the accident. There, I often questioned God about what He was doing with my life and why. Yet with every visit, I also marveled at His mercy in sparing my life.

On this particular visit, I deepened my commitment to Jesus, vowing my life to serve Him, whatever that may be and wherever He may lead.

With a renewed spirit, I continued to Dr. Graham's office.

Entering the waiting room, I quietly whispered, "I give myself to You, Jesus." This visit was my first without expectations. I simply wanted to be all God wanted me to be—whatever that was. I felt no anxiety about what may come; I only felt my heavenly Father's great peace, presence, and love.

After assessing my multitude of injuries, Dr. Graham proceeded with the routine X-rays of my ankle and then carefully positioned them on the viewing screen. He studied them in prolonged silence, yet I remained at peace.

When he eventually spoke, his tone was just above a whisper. "Your ankle is healing, Dale." He shook his head. "The blood has started circulating again." His voice held a quiet awe that permeated the room. The pause that followed was our stunned silence.

He then pointed to the screen, eyes wide with curiosity and disbelief. "I don't understand it," he whispered. He looked down at the floor momentarily, then back at the X-rays. "I can't explain it, Dale." He slowly shook his head in disbelief, his eyes locked with mine, searching my face for an answer. I knew the answer.

Dr. Graham continued, "Your ankle has healed more in the past two weeks than in the last six months combined! I just don't understand it. . . ."

In the quiet amazement, there was a resounding echo deep in my spirit: "He who loses his life for My sake will find it" (Matthew 10:39).

I'm thrilled to share that within a few months following this life-changing event, I was out of my cast and learning to walk.

First things first; full surrender, walking by faith.

Eventually, I regained full mobility. I could run, participate in many sports, and, yes, continue my pursuit to become a professional airline pilot—all without a noticeable limp or further surgeries, now for almost fifty years.

A powerful principle of God is doing things in sensical order to ensure the best outcome. Thoughtfully and logically, ask yourself, *What comes first? Second? Next?*

When building a house, laying a solid foundation and floor must come first to support the next step—the walls, which need to be firmly secured to the foundation before adding the roof.

If the foundation falters, how can we securely build on it?

Faith is a foundational force. The power of faith as a verb allows followers of Jesus Christ to *do* as Jesus did.

He taught His followers to pray, "Your will be done on Earth as it is in Heaven" (Matthew 6:10).

Jesus is saying to us: Whatever is happening in Heaven can happen in your life.

How? By faith.

Pause and imagine the power of Heaven on Earth in your daily life and challenges.

Faith is acting on what you believe.

Jesus reveals this level of power through His multiple spoken promises, such as these:

> "He who believes in Me, the works that I do he will do also; and greater works than these he will do, because I go to My Father. And whatever you ask in My name, that I will do, that the Father may be glorified in the Son. If you ask anything in My name, I will do it." — John 14:12–14

"All things are possible to him who believes." — Mark 9:23

"If you have faith as a mustard seed, you will say to this mountain, 'Move from here to there,' and it will move; and nothing will be impossible for you." — Matthew 17:20

"Whatever things you ask in prayer, believing, you will receive." — Matthew 21:22

"According to your faith let it be to you." — Matthew 9:29

Imagine living with the confidence that your prayers are not only heard but answered.

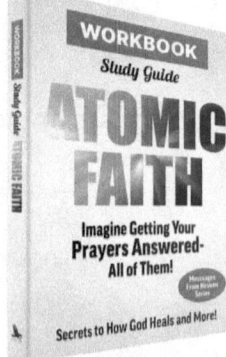

Chapter 4

THE STORY OF TWO PARALLEL LIVES

"According to your faith let it *be* to you."
— Matthew 9:29 (author emphasis)

W E NOW UNDERSTAND THAT WE WILL NOT RECEIVE HEALING SIMPLY BECAUSE GOD *CAN* HEAL. Nor will we see miracles because God *can* do miracles. We become healed and see miracles when we take action with atomic *faith* in what we know is true from God's Word. His Word is truth (John 17:17).

God *can* heal—but will He? Let's look at the following illustration of how belief and faith work differently but together.

Belief and Faith Are Two Sides of the Same Coin

Visualize holding an official US silver dollar. Its value is one dollar. Created and authorized by the US Treasury as legal tender, the coin is tradeable for goods and services on the open economic market.

One side of the 2024 Morgan and Peace silver dollar is stamped with an emblem of Lady Liberty's head. The opposite side is stamped with the emblem of the US federal bird—an eagle.

Though the coin is legal tender, its value is conditional. Both sides must be *intact* to be spendable. If I were to put either side of the coin against a grinder, removing the stamped emblem, the coin would become only a shiny piece of worthless metal, its power for trade lost.

A merchant is not obligated to accept a defaced coin, as *both* sides must be intact as created to hold legal, tradeable value. The treasury department did not deface the coin—I did, robbing myself of its original value and intended use.

Consider the illustration from Heaven's viewpoint. God created an open spiritual market with specifically stamped tender. Imagine that His two-sided coin (so to speak) can be spent on the spiritual market for goods and services.

The two sides of Heaven's spiritual coin are distinctively different: one side represents *belief*, and the other represents *faith*. Just as an earthly silver dollar must remain as created to retain its power of trade, so must the two sides of God's created heavenly coin. Both belief and faith must be present to maintain spiritual power for answered prayers.

Belief and faith are like legal tender for answered prayer.

We can hold an earthly coin in our hands with *hope* that others will accept it for trade, but the currency must be used according to the rules of its creator, the US Treasury.

Likewise, in God's marketplace, we must adhere to His rules (His Word) and correctly utilize *belief and faith* in our quest for answered prayer.

Imagine walking into a grocery store in the US and trying to pay with foreign currency. You couldn't buy groceries because the store is set up to accept only US dollars. Similarly, we cannot approach God with any "currency" not authorized by His Word and expect to receive an answer from Heaven.

To bring Heaven's will to Earth, the spiritual coin's two distinguishing sides—belief and faith—must work together as God designed.

If we eliminate either aspect of God's economic tender, we cannot have confidence in receiving answers to prayer.

The biblical difference between hope, belief, and faith is depicted in the following story, which I witnessed personally, as did hundreds of others.

The illustration deals with life-and-death challenges. My intention is not to blame anyone, hurt anyone's feelings, or cause other discomforts. My heart is to share the story with sensitivity and responsibility as a learning opportunity.

The real-life experience can potentially help many readers as we analyze—from Heaven's perspective—what actions were taken according to Jesus's teaching and what could have been improved.

While working as an airline pilot instructor for forty years, I often cited airplane crashes as teaching tools to train pilots on safety and the importance of learning from the experiences of others. We carefully examined what went right and wrong in various aircraft accidents, focusing on understanding rather than placing blame. After all, everyone makes mistakes, and each one offers valuable lessons.

Just as aviation accident prevention teaches us principles to improve safety, we can apply similar insights to real-life situations. One of the most impactful lessons I've learned is summed up in this phrase: "Wise people learn from experience, but wiser people learn from the experiences of others."

The following story offers powerful lessons from someone else's life-and-death experience.

The Story of Two Parallel Lives

Two women had terminal cancer at the same time, but each took a different path. By exploring Helen's and Margie's paths, we unlock the hidden biblical keys of God's power and gain profound insights into how He heals.

As we covered in the previous chapter, hope, belief, and faith are similar yet distinctly different. Each must be understood and used in its proper order and context to receive answers to prayer.

Helen had been like an aunt to me and her children as though they were my cousins. She and her family were deeply rooted in our church, and we were incredibly close.

Helen had been a devout follower of Jesus since childhood. Unfortunately, in her late fifties, she was diagnosed with terminal breast cancer that spread to her liver. Despite prayers for healing, Helen's condition worsened. Her last year was particularly tough. The pastor visited her weekly and prayed for her, and she was anointed with oil several times. But her situation worsened.

Her daily prayer partner was Margie, who was in her thirties, lived about five miles from Helen, and was a new believer. She also attended the same church, a close-knit community of about eight hundred members who excelled in fellowship and church life.

Margie had been following Jesus for just over a year when, sadly, she was also diagnosed with terminal breast cancer, which later metastasized to her brain and lungs. Surgery was no longer an option.

Margie was also receiving regular visits and prayers from the pastor as the two friends faced their final stages of life. Both situations were dire.

As a newer believer, Margie looked up to Helen, seeing her as a model of Christian devotion. They shared a strong bond, enhanced by their similar struggles with terminal cancer. Due to their harsh circumstances, they nurtured their friendship primarily over the phone, praying together daily and supporting each other.

Both women believed in salvation through Jesus Christ, acknowledged Him as the Messiah, and believed the Bible was the infallible Word of God. Each had unshakable faith, found joy in the Lord, were secure in their salvation, and firmly believed they were heaven-bound.

They also shared a deep belief in God's *power* to heal and believed the accounts of miracles in the Bible. Each believed God *could* heal—if that was His will—and they prayed fervently for healing. Their *hope* for personal healing remained strong, having been prayed for many times.

Both women's beliefs were based on Christian church teachings. They rightly believed that when God doesn't heal, His love and faithfulness to His promises don't diminish. However, they incorrectly believed that God chooses to heal some people but not others.

The prevailing teaching was that while God *can* heal, He remains sovereign, not always intervening in the ways we hope or expect. This teaching had shaped the church family's understanding, tempering their belief in healing and thereby robbing them of the supernatural power of faith.

Although Helen believed God *could* heal, she did not express a firm belief that God would heal *her*.

Margie reasoned that if God did not heal Helen—a devout and established church member—why would He heal her, a newer Christian? The thought troubled her. She felt that Helen deserved healing more than she did.

I recalled the days, weeks, and months following my plane crash. I had dug into the Bible and begun learning and practicing the secrets to healing that God had provided for everyone. I hoped Helen and Margie would experience the supernatural healing I had received.

My Visit with Helen

I reached out to Helen several times throughout her difficult last year. Lovingly, I shared with her the differences

I had discovered between *belief* and *faith* following the plane crash.

She was alert and listened with interest as I then shared insights that had helped me regain my ability to walk, see from my seriously damaged eye, and recover from back, head, and multiple other injuries.

I also shared Scriptures about healing and God's promises, hoping the verses would bolster Helen from hope to belief and then into taking action by faith. However, she wasn't fully receptive to some of Jesus's teachings—those that were outside the traditions of the church she had attended her entire life.

Helen confirmed caringly to me that God *could* heal, but she still doubted He *would*. Her condition was worsening; therefore, she reasoned that it was likely she would experience the same outcome as many cancer patients before her.

My heart was pained.

She hoped for a miracle but lingered in *hope*, continuing to struggle with *belief* in the integrity of God's healing promises. Having not yet anchored her belief in the promise that Jesus had already provided her healing, she was unable to exercise *faith* in that truth.

A few minutes later, Helen was visibly exhausted, too worn out to be willing to reconsider her understanding of the difference between belief and faith, as Jesus had taught. I left her side and her home feeling a stronger bond of love, yet deeply saddened.

Several more times, I visited my precious friend and her family, who consistently welcomed me with open arms.

Each visit, I saw that Helen's health had further declined. My heart grew heavier, knowing God had a much better way.

In her final days, Helen appeared resigned to her impending death. Hope was gone.

On my last visit, knowing I would likely not see my dear friend alive again on this side of Heaven, I kissed her forehead and said my goodbyes. I rejoiced that Heaven was her eternal destination, yet I felt grieved that her departure would be earlier than God's best.

Helen passed away at age sixty-one. Her funeral was glorious. Her life had left a legacy of good for her family, friends, and church for God's glory. She was loved and respected by all who knew her.

Though she lost her battle with cancer, she won the war over her eternal destination. She finished her earthly race as a child of God through Jesus Christ and was safe and secure in her heavenly home.

At her funeral, many repeated an all-too-familiar but untrue statement. "It was her time to go." But in my heart, I knew Helen had departed far too soon. Others said, "Heaven needs her more than we need her here on Earth."

The comment grieved me. Yes, Helen was in Heaven, but the world needed her light and voice more than Heaven did. Heaven was her *reward*, but this Earth was where Jesus wanted to live *through* her to continue touching lives until her work was fully complete.

That experience reminded me, yet again, that if we desire to receive God's best, we cannot delay in developing our faith.

Building a house during a storm is difficult. Building a solid foundation of faith before the storms of life hit is much more effective.

"Therefore whoever hears these sayings of Mine, and does them, I will liken him to a wise man who built his house on the rock: and the rain descended, the floods came, and the winds blew and beat on that house; and it did not fall, for it was founded on the rock.

"But everyone who hears these sayings of Mine, and does not do them, will be like a foolish man who built his house on the sand: and the rain descended, the floods came, and the winds blew and beat on that house; and it fell. And great was its fall." — Matthew 7:24–27

Though Helen's story was full of love, respect, dignity, and grace, her life ended unnecessarily early. God's perfect will was not for Helen to enter Heaven because of a bout with cancer at age sixty-one. He had made provision for her healing. It was His best for Helen to overcome through spiritual growth. However, His permissive will allowed an outcome based on her choices.

Paula's Visit with Margie

Margie was devastated by Helen's death. She believed that since God hadn't healed Helen, He certainly wouldn't heal her. She was suffering from severe depression and had all but given up on any hope of living.

Just as the Spirit of God had prompted me to visit Helen, He led my wonderful wife, Paula, to visit Margie. Through our prayers and sharing Jesus's teachings, we hoped Margie would understand that God's desire was to heal her and that she would recognize the importance of using her active faith.

Paula called the hospital and reached Margie's sister, who cautioned, "Margie doesn't want visitors because she's embarrassed by her appearance. And she doesn't have the strength or desire to pull herself together because of her severe depression. But please come." The entire family felt that Margie had only a few days to live.

At Margie's bedside in hospice, Paula was taken aback by her sickly, weak, and discolored condition. It was no surprise that doctors and all of her family didn't expect her to live long enough to see the weekend.

Paula comforted Margie with a warm, loving greeting, affirming God's love for her. Then she reached out and gently held Margie's hand.

Smiling, Paula shared about the family of God, the attributes of heavenly life that await us, and the incredibly wonderful future believers have in Jesus.

Paula then asked Margie, "May I read from the Bible?"

"Of course," Margie whispered.

Paula shared Scripture about the integrity of God's faithfulness to His promises: He has the power to heal, but we must first have hope for healing. Then we must establish belief in our hearts that His will is to heal, and believe that

His will and His Word are the same. Softly, she stressed, "Healing is for you, Margie, today, now."

Paula explained the differences between hope, belief, and faith. She clarified that belief comes from knowing what God has promised and then putting absolute confidence in that promise. "We don't believe or have faith in ourselves," she explained. "We believe what God promised—what He has said and demonstrated in the Bible. When we accept God's Word as His will, our confidence in His promises is anchored in our hearts. Then, when hope and belief are established, the next step is taking action in faith." She clarified, "Faith is *acting on* what you believe. It's faith that opens the channel to God's power. It's faith that brings Heaven to Earth. It's through our faith that we receive healing."

Margie was confused about the teaching because God hadn't healed Helen. "Why would God heal me? He didn't heal Helen—and she was so much more deserving than me."

Paula placed her warm hand on Margie's cool arm and leaned close to her ear. She whispered, "God does not show favoritism; healing is based on what Jesus accomplished on the cross—for everyone. He offers salvation, healing, and all His blessings to any who believes and acts on that belief with faith."

She gently squeezed Margie's arm in reassurance. "God's will is to heal everyone, just as His will is to save everyone. Jesus never once turned anyone down who asked to be saved or healed." Softly and lovingly, Paula said, "Let's consider what the Bible says in Matthew 9:22. Jesus said, 'Be of good cheer, daughter; your faith has made you well.'"

Two precious hours together had passed, discussing hope, belief, and faith, reviewing many promises from the Bible, and praying for Margie's physical healing. Paula took Margie's hand and squeezed it. "Margie, God has a plan for your life. He wants you to believe His Word is true. He has given each of us free will to choose. He said in Deuteronomy 30:19, 'I have set before you life and death, blessing and cursing; therefore choose life, that both you and your descendants may live.'"

Paula continued, "Remember, your faith grows as you hear God's promises. Read the Scriptures out loud to yourself." She handed her a page of Bible verses. "Read them over and over. You've been programmed to think a certain way, but you need to realign your beliefs with God and His Word. Reading them aloud is the key to building the kind of faith that will transform your life and bring healing to your body."

As Paula stood to leave, she looked into Margie's eyes, smiling, and added, "Margie, God's given you the choice. I pray you will choose His best. A lot of people love you. Why not choose life?"

The next day, when the doctor arrived to check on Margie, she said, "It's okay, doctor. I'm fine now. A friend came to visit yesterday and prayed for me. God touched me, and I believe I'm okay now."

The doctor smiled at Margie. "I'm glad you're feeling better today."

Several days later, doctors were stunned to see Margie's condition improving dramatically. Within a week, she spoke enthusiastically to Paula over the phone. "They could find no trace of cancer in my body! My faith is *now*. My healing is *now*. It's *done*. God answered my prayers of faith. God healed me!"

Eight days after Paula's visit, Margie walked out of hospice on her own, her physical strength renewed—cancer-free. She exemplified Jesus's teaching from Matthew 9:29, "According to *your faith* let it *be to you*" (author emphasis).

In hospice, at the brink of death, Margie had come to understand that hope and belief are not the same as faith. But together, they are key ingredients to unlocking God's power for answered prayer.

While this story may sound unbelievable, it's as true as anything I've ever witnessed. Margie's healing is another testament to the power of atomic faith and the truth of God's Word.

Faith is acting on what you believe.

I'll never forget the amazing celebration between Paula and Margie thirty years after Margie walked out of hospice cancer-free. What a beautiful, joyous experience. Margie had unlocked the secrets to how God heals. She had learned how to use atomic faith.

Many people in the Bible were healed by following Jesus's instruction, "according to *your faith*" (Matthew 9:29, author emphasis).

We know from God's Word that healing is His will and available to us. Long before Jesus's ministry on Earth, an

Old Testament prophet proclaimed God's promise: "By His stripes we *are* healed" (Isaiah 53:5, author emphasis).

After Jesus's death and resurrection, the apostle Peter stated, "By whose stripes you *were* healed" (1 Peter 2:24, author emphasis).

Both statements are true—the first is a present-tense promise, and the other is a past-tense declaration, both referring to what Jesus has already provided.

These verses make clear that Jesus provided what is needed and emphasize that God shows no favoritism. His healing is for you, me, Joe across the street, Donna down the block—anyone in any condition who believes with active faith what God has provided.

God's character is consistent; His Word does not change; He is the same yesterday, today, and forever. His unchanging will is to heal "all your diseases" (Psalm 103:3).

Miracle healing from God is a process:

- The path begins with hope (desired outcome).
- Belief matures from hope (firmly rooted agreement with God and His Word).
- Faith is acting on what you believe (speaking and taking action in agreement with what's in your heart).

When you take action in faith, it ultimately brings to pass what you are believing for.

Helen's and Margie's journeys began with hope. Both knew God as their Savior and *hoped* He would be their Healer. Both agreed that God *could* heal, but they questioned *if* healing was His will for them.

Their difficulty was in progressing from hope to belief in what is trustworthy and unchangeable—God's Word:

God *is* our Healer, just as He *is* our Savior.

Jesus has provided salvation for everyone, in any condition, who believes in Him. *But will they choose to be saved?*

Likewise, God has provided healing for everyone, in any condition, who acts on what they believe. *But will they choose to be healed?*

Those are the big questions. The quick answer is no, not without *faith*. Faith connects God's promises and Heaven's power to our prayers.

Atomic faith is acting on what you believe that agrees with God's Word.

Hosea 4:6 says, "My people are destroyed for lack of knowledge." The Scripture verse means that ignorance about God and His ways can lead to harm and destruction.

We Don't Know What We Don't Know

A lot of people believe they understand what faith is. I've met many who say they live by faith every day. But if we were to take a closer look at how they actually live, something becomes clear—people often don't realize how much they *don't* know. It's a common struggle we all face as human beings.

Over the years, while traveling around the world, I've seen this again and again. But what's even more concerning is when someone *thinks* they know something they really don't. This can make a person hard to teach—especially if they've spent years learning things that aren't quite true.

When someone has been taught incorrectly or has believed something based on faulty teaching, they're usually not quick to accept a different point of view. This can happen to any of us. That's why it's so important to regularly read the Bible. When we do, the Holy Spirit can show us where our beliefs don't line up with God's Word.

The Bible tells us to keep renewing our minds so we can learn to think the way God does. The world around us is constantly shaping our beliefs, often in ways that go against what God says is true. "Do not be conformed to this world, but be transformed by the renewing of your mind" (Romans 12:2).

Changing how we think isn't easy. But the purpose of this book is to help guide you in that process—so you can begin thinking and living the way God intends, according to His Word.

In this chapter, we've drawn clear distinctions between hope, belief, and faith. Through illustrations, we've demonstrated that faith and belief are like two sides of the same coin—different but working together. We've also come to understand that healing doesn't happen simply because God has the power to heal. Likewise, miracles don't occur solely because God is capable of performing them.

When we act in faith on the beliefs in our hearts that agree with God's Word, we unlock the power of Heaven, where the impossible becomes possible.

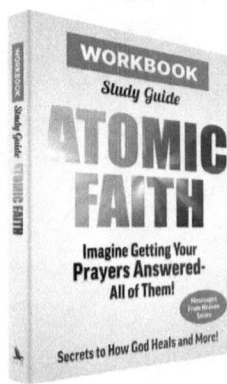

Chapter 5

HOPE: THE BLUEPRINT OF FAITH

THE AMELIA EARHART STORY

Now faith is the substance of things hoped
for, the evidence of things not seen.
— Hebrews 11:1

IN HEAVEN, THERE IS A GREAT DEAL OF DIFFERENCE
BETWEEN *HOPE*, *BELIEF*, AND *FAITH*, THEREBY MAKING A
DIFFERENCE ON EARTH. All three words are found frequently
in the Bible, and each plays an essential role in receiving
answers to our prayers. However, they are a part of a larger
whole, and all three are required to get the results we desire.

Without understanding the differences between hope,
belief, and faith, our prayers are hindered or delayed.
Often the answers never come, and God is not to blame.
We are. When we use the knowledge God has provided

in His Word, we thrive. When we neglect His directives, principles, and promises, we leave ourselves vulnerable to the enemy. If we continue in neglect, we're staying on the path to our downfall.

> "My people are destroyed for lack of knowledge."
> — Hosea 4:6

Our spiritual lives barely get off the ground until we align our thinking and desires with God's character and Word—which is how Heaven operates. Our prayers will stall if we're not interacting correctly with hope, belief, and faith.

God's way is always the best way.

Our accurate understanding of hope, belief, and faith matters. God gave these forces to all people for our blessing. We can use them with our own strength—*natural faith*—and get a degree of benefit. The result may be impressive, but that earthly faith is limited by what we can accomplish in the natural realm.

The alternative is to utilize the three forces God's way: with atomic faith—*supernatural faith*, which provides supernatural results.

Natural and supernatural faith produce results; however, the difference is in the quality and measure of the results. Let's review the definitions and differences by way of examples:

Natural faith is a limited force that releases natural power. Think of natural faith as a conventional bomb. When detonated, the explosive power to its intended target is limited. The force can be impressive, even extraordinary, which we'll see through an incredible real-life example in this chapter. However, the power of natural faith to bring substantially greater results—like answered prayers— remains limited to what is naturally possible.

Natural faith makes what is already possible more likely.

Supernatural faith is an unlimited force that releases unlimited power based on God's living Word. Let's view that power as an atomic bomb: far superior in power to create change than conventional explosives. The power of supernatural faith to bring epic results—like answered prayers—is unlimited, beyond what is natural, which is why I call it *atomic faith.* Such faith has no boundaries against its power and creative ability.

Supernatural faith makes the impossible possible.

Consider the miracle of my ankle in Chapter 1. Hope, belief, and faith were applied according to God's design, bringing about supernatural results. The outcome defied medical explanation. Atomic faith achieved what was impossible in the natural world.

The following illustration is shared to simplify the principles of natural hope, belief, and faith.

The Amelia Earhart Story—An Example of Natural Faith

Throughout my life, I've been deeply inspired by Amelia Earhart's exceptional life. Her natural hope, belief, and faith advanced aviation in profound ways. She was the first woman to fly solo across the Atlantic Ocean. She set numerous aviation records and became a predominant voice in promoting commercial air travel.

Her ambitious goal was to become the first woman to fly around the world as the pilot of a private aircraft. Driven to achieve what no woman had before, she and her accomplishments are honored at the Portal of the Folded Wings monument in Burbank, California.

Ms. Earhart relied on her natural faith to successfully complete a solo transatlantic flight from the US to Europe.

In the 1930s, airplanes were notoriously unreliable and dangerous, making her historic overwater journey incredibly risky. Weather was often unpredictable, and navigation depended on magnetic compasses, which were prone to error. With such extreme limitations and dangers, what was her contingency plan if her engine failed over the open ocean—the same treacherous waters that had claimed the lives of *Titanic* passengers?

Despite thorough planning, her flight required faith.

After a harrowing fourteen-hour and fifty-six-minute flight across the perilous Atlantic, she landed in a pasture in Northern Ireland. As the story goes, a farmhand, likely astonished, asked her if she'd flown far. With a great sense of victory, we imagine, and perhaps a hearty laugh, she replied, "From America."

Ms. Earhart's Atlantic crossing exemplifies the essence of natural hope, belief, and natural faith, proving her to be one of the most inspirational figures in American history. As we see, extraordinary results are possible with natural faith, but it does not make the impossible possible.

Amelia was not only an aviation pioneer but gained celebrity status. She met presidents, championed women's rights, and became a cultural icon. She wrote best-selling books about her flying adventures and helped establish the Ninety-Nines, an organization for female pilots.

Her passion for flying started when she was young, with her first flight experience at Daugherty Field in Long Beach, California. That flight changed her life. She said, "By the time I had got two or three hundred feet off the ground . . . I knew I had to fly."[5]

Interestingly, my aviation journey also began at Daugherty Field, where I accumulated over five thousand takeoffs and landings.

Within the Portal of the Folded Wings mausoleum, Ms. Earhart's memorial plaque hangs head to toe with mine. I feel great awe and honor each time I visit.

(Perhaps aviation's most ironic airplane crash is the one described in its entirety in my autobiographical book *Flight To Heaven*.)

Portal of the Folded Wings, Valhalla Memorial Cemetery. Site of Dale Black's sole-survivor airplane crash into the top of the dome at 135 mph and the subsequent 100-foot free fall of the three pilots to the ground.

Photo taken thirty minutes after the crash. Two firefighters examine the wreckage near the aircraft's engine at the base of the Portal of the Folded Wings Mausoleum.

Fate, Coincidence or Cruel Irony? *Arrow points to the top of the 100-foot-high memorial to dead aviators where the twin-engine plane struck after its takeoff from Hollywood-Burbank Airport. Two men were killed. A third pilot was taken to St. Joseph's Hospital in critical condition.*
July 18, 1969.
Photo by Harold Morby from KMPC AirWatch

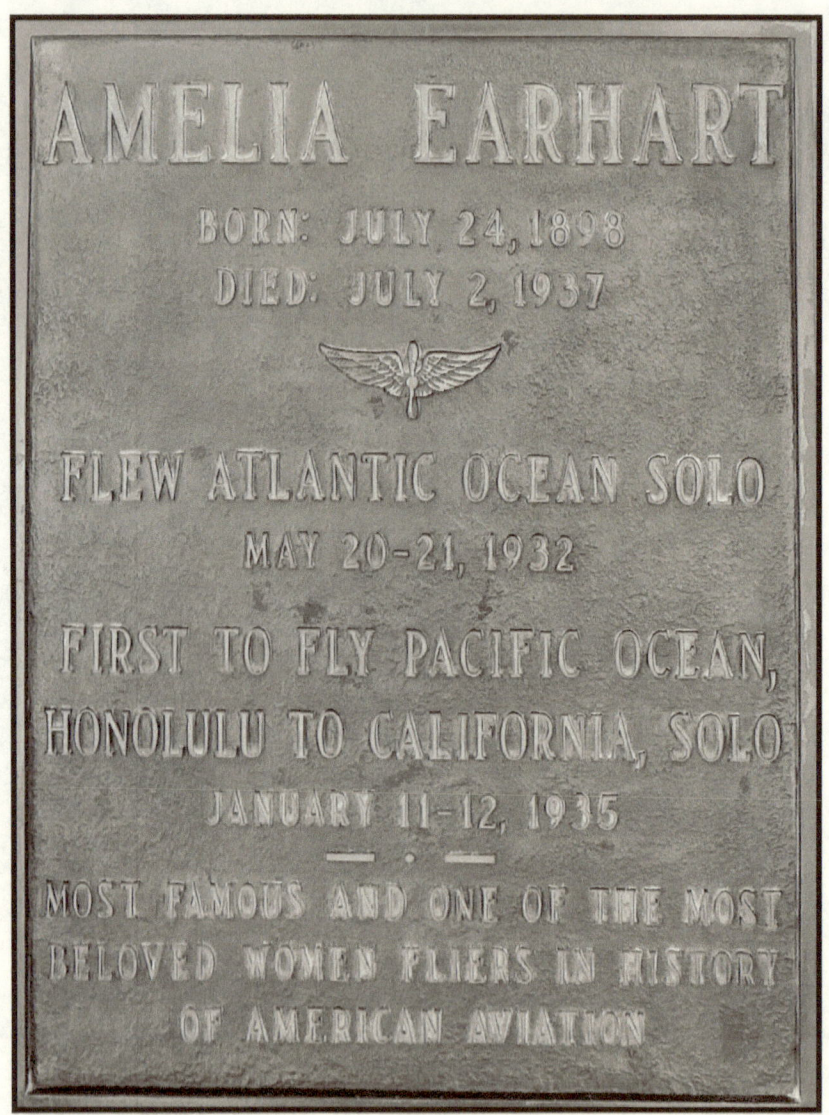

Amelia Earhart Memorial Plaque

Dale Black's plaque was installed in the Portal of the Folded Wings on the fiftieth anniversary of the crash.

Ms. Earhart's amazing story illustrates the workings of natural hope, belief, and faith.

Young Amelia was deeply inspired by Charles Lindbergh's historic flight. His achievement of natural faith planted in her a seed of *hope* that she too could make her mark in the skies with her own groundbreaking nonstop solo flight across the Atlantic.

Amelia Earhart's amazing journey of natural faith began with hope, which she quickly fanned into her *belief* that she could fulfill her dream. Her belief was in her earthly piloting skills and experience, the reliability of her aircraft, and confidence in weather forecasts. Together, these natural factors strengthened her natural belief in the success of her flight.

In 1932, the culmination of Ms. Earhart's efforts took flight from Harbor Grace, Newfoundland, Canada. She piloted a red Lockheed Vega alone, her aspirations soaring into natural *faith*. She had progressed from hope to belief to actions of faith.

Once faith is activated, resistance is never far behind.

Ms. Earhart faced formidable challenges during her flight, including strong winds, icy conditions, and mechanical troubles. But her resolve never wavered. Although her destination was not yet visible, she held on tightly to natural faith, persisting through every challenge until she saw her desire realized.

She landed safely in Europe as the first female pilot to achieve a transatlantic solo fight. As it turned out, she's been the only person who made that flight since Lindbergh.

Let's explore the forces—hope, belief, and faith— together, beginning with hope. Step by step, we'll move from hope to a better grasp of belief, and finally to a deeper understanding of faith.

Hope Is Not Faith

Definitions for *hope* make clear that hope is different from faith. Hope means "to expect with confidence"[6] and "to cherish a desire with anticipation."[7] We see these modeled in Ms. Earhart's aviation expedition.

Hope is *essential* to our lives and fundamental to our human design, as we read in 1 Corinthians 13:13: "Now abide faith, *hope*, love"(author emphasis). Without hope, daily living is miserable. Wouldn't you agree?

Hope Is the Blueprint of Faith

Hope is *not* faith. Not even close. Hope is the blueprint of faith—the image in Ms. Earhart's heart and mind of what she desired. But hope is not what caused her dream to come to pass, just as a building's blueprint does *not* erect the building. But try constructing a building without a blueprint. The resulting structure will likely be sloppy, ugly, impractical, and unsafe.

As the blueprint for your faith, hope is the image in your heart of what you desire. It's the beginning of your journey from desire to realization.

Ms. Earhart's successful solo flight across the Atlantic wasn't achieved through hope alone. Her hope served as the foundation rooted in her meticulous preflight planning. Hope evolved into belief as she carefully attended to every detail—selecting the right aircraft, charting her flight path, and gathering the necessary supplies. By transforming her hope into a well-thought-out plan, she created something she could truly then *believe* in.

For prayers to be answered, hope is first required—whether hope for healing, provision, deliverance, peace, security, or whatever you desire.

But *hope* is not belief, and hope is not faith. Hope is the *starting point*, the focused desire in your heart, the planning stage.

Hope is the blueprint of faith.

As I shared earlier, having been a longtime, passionate airline pilot-instructor, I often use aviation illustrations. So in the following three sections, we'll unlock the differences between the workings of hope, belief, and faith by planning a trip together, taking the steps to fulfill the plan, and then taking the flight to our destination.

Hope Is Like the "Preflight"

Hope is not the flight itself; hope is our flight *plan* and preflight choices—our starting point, our desired *expectation* for the specific flight.

- ✓ In hope, we select our desired destination.
- ✓ In hope, I inspect the aircraft and make sure it's airworthy while you, in hope, make your plans from home and start packing.
- ✓ In hope, I check the weather—as do you, to choose what to pack.
- ✓ In hope, I calculate the fuel, flight time, and costs.
- ✓ In hope, the fuel and luggage are loaded, and you and the other passengers are boarding.
- ✓ In hope, we visualize the entire flight. I assess the variables and contingencies of the flight while you envision the view you'll have above the clouds.
- ✓ In hope, I check the flight control systems and set up all avionics according to the selected navigation airways, and, in hope, you stow your carry-on and settle in your seat.

As we saw, the preflight planning is *not* the flight itself. Before I start the engines and you order your in-flight beverage, we take the preflight steps for the flight we *hope* to take.

Belief Is Like the Plane "Taxiing"

The *belief* that you will acquire something—the flight—is a deeper, greater conviction than hope.

- ✓ In belief, I file the flight plan with the authorities.
- ✓ In belief, I take action to start the engines, and you buckle up.
- ✓ In belief, I radio the control tower for permission to push back, taxi to the runway, and start the takeoff roll.

✓ In belief, I advance power levers and accelerate to takeoff speed.

✓ In belief, I apply takeoff thrust.

✓ In belief, you and your companions talk about the destination, further enthused by the engines' vibrations and roar.

Though the noise and vibrations are loud, our *belief* is not yet *faith*. We are actively in belief mode but still on the ground. Yet this aircraft is designed to fly. It must fly to reach the destination.

In belief, I've taken care of the preliminaries that will move us into faith. Everything I've done thus far is mandatory for flight but still *limiting* our flight. We're not yet airborne.

Faith Is Like the "Flight"

Hope started the process. Then our hearts moved into *believing in* the reality of the flight. Our belief was made evident by starting the active engines, taxiing out for takeoff, and beginning the race down the runway, accelerating.

✓ In faith, I lift the jet into the air, climbing to fly above the clouds and weather. In faith, you're confident I know what I'm doing as your pilot.

✓ In faith, I raise the landing gear and bring the flaps up incrementally.

✓ In faith, I increase our speed: 180 knots for liftoff, 250 knots for climb, 316 knots for climb to cruising altitude.

✓ In faith, we're now cruising at 547 knots. You've pulled out your paperback in faith that . . . we're flying toward our destination!

That's *faith in action.*

We began our trip with expectant hope, moved into firm belief, and then took off into active faith.

Though hope, belief, and faith are each distinct, each plays an essential role in receiving answers to our prayers.

Belief vs. Faith

You've likely heard and used the words *belief* and *believe.* So let me ask you this: Have you perhaps thought that the meanings of belief and faith are very similar and possibly interchangeable?

If you're like most people, you've probably misunderstood the distinct differences between belief and faith, causing you to misuse these two dynamic words. Not understanding their unique roles is another reason why prayers go unanswered. For example, most people believe God *can* heal, yet they're dying (physically or emotionally), much like those who have misplaced faith or have no faith at all.

Their *belief* that God *can* and does heal is correct. But the Bible tells us, "By whose stripes you *were* healed" (1 Peter 2:24, author emphasis).

"Were" is past tense—a done deal. We are not required to wait for Jesus to do something more after we've presented our requests to God in prayer. Our answer is already available and ready for us to receive. We tap into God's power by believing His Word is true (John 17:17)

101

and believing with faith—supernatural faith—that we *have already* received what God has provided.

In this chapter, we explored the differences between hope, belief, and faith, using aviation as an example of natural faith in action.

- Hope is like "the preflight."
- Belief is like "the taxi."
- Faith is like "the flight."

We distinguished that natural faith is a limited force and supernatural faith, what I call atomic faith, has no limits. Supernatural faith is the kind of faith that can transform your life and change the world.

Supernatural faith begins with hope, grows into a strong belief in God's Word, and culminates in acting on that belief.

Faith is acting on what you believe.

PART THREE

How Faith Works

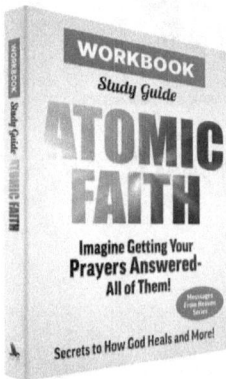

Chapter 6

THE HAUNTED HOUSE ON MARBLE LANE

"Behold, I give you the authority to
trample on serpents and scorpions, and
over all the power of the enemy, and
nothing shall by any means hurt you."
— Luke 10:19

To those who believe in Jesus as their Lord and Savior, He gives His authority and power. We see evidence of this promise through the work of His disciples. They clearly demonstrated His power to disarm demons.

Because God and His Word are unchangeable, we know His power is still available today through the Holy Spirit in His followers. His power in us is just as effective as in Jesus's ministry on Earth.

However, to utilize that supernatural authority most effectively, one needs a basic understanding of spiritual warfare, demons, and the kingdom of darkness.

The kingdom of darkness is what stands between you and answered prayer.

This chapter covers the basics of spiritual warfare. I've written a more detailed book focused on demons, your invisible enemy, that includes more specifics about spiritual warfare. That book is intended to be part of the *Messages from Heaven Series.*

Satan tries to block our prayers by using his demonic forces to interfere. But if we know how to take authority by faith in Jesus's name, we clear the way for answered prayers. Lacking understanding of faith and how it works as a spiritual weapon will likely delay the answers. *Faith* is the tool God gave us to open Heaven's channel for His will to come to Earth.

Consider Daniel's prayer from the Old Testament. He prayed and fasted in faith for an answer from God. But the spiritual prince of Persia—a strong demonic angel— fought to keep that answer from getting through to him (Daniel 10:13). In response to Daniel's faith and diligence, God sent reinforcements to help defeat the principalities interfering with the delivery of God's answer.

On Earth, we continuously live within a spiritual battle zone.

Discounting the spiritual battle we live in leaves us vulnerable to becoming victims of satan's schemes and frustrated by unanswered prayers.

The apostle Paul wrote about the spiritual war zone and who we fight against. Our enemy is not people; our enemy is spiritual powers operating in this world's kingdom (satan's). The evil beings we're battling—whether we're fighting or not—are satan's agents, and their assignment is to stand against God and God's people.

> We do not wrestle against flesh and blood, but against principalities, against powers, against the rulers of the darkness of this age, against spiritual hosts of wickedness in the heavenly places.
> — Ephesians 6:12

Be aware of this: Spiritual warfare is involved in everything we pray for. So we must understand our enemy and how Jesus taught us to handle satan and his demons.

Dealing with satan demands that we understand the authority Jesus has given us.

Engaging Demonic Forces With the Written Word

Satan knows who poses a threat to his kingdom: potentially every follower of Jesus. Sadly, many are untaught. They don't know how to fight with spiritual weapons and don't understand that they (we all) live in a spiritual battle zone that spills into their natural lives.

We have been given access to Jesus's authority over *all* of the enemy's power. However, to engage that power and overcome satan, we must *believe* Jesus's Word is true and take action in *faith* based on His Word.

The Bible's account of Daniel seeking an answer to prayer offers an excellent example of how to ask God for something and what we can expect in response.

> I set my face toward the Lord God to make request by prayer and supplications, with fasting, sackcloth, and ashes. And I prayed to the Lord my God, and made confession, and said, "O Lord, great and awesome God, who keeps His covenant and mercy with those who love Him, and with those who keep His commandments." — Daniel 9:3–4

Daniel was repenting not only for himself but for all of God's people. As he confessed and repented, he also praised and worshipped God (vv. 5–20). This part of the illustration takes us back to Chapter 3 of *Atomic Faith*, putting first things first: seeking God and His righteousness.

Next, Daniel asked God for an answer about the outcome of His people in captivity. Daniel's prayer caused the spiritual battle to begin. Twenty-one days passed without an answer. What did Daniel do during that time? He *persistently* prayed, fasted, confessed sin, and worshipped the Lord *until* he received an answer.

The Bible tells us that God sent the angel Gabriel with the answer as soon as Daniel prayed. Yet Daniel did not receive that answer for twenty-one days. Why? What happened?

Resistance occurred in the heavenlies (Earth's atmosphere). In an attempt to keep Daniel's prayer from being answered, a battle raged between satan's evil angels and God's messenger angel.

With atomic faith, Daniel persisted in repenting and praising God. He continued steadfastly with faith for his answer . . . until the answer arrived.

Yet how easy it is for us to give up when we don't receive quick answers. How often does doubt enter, robbing our faith and sabotaging the answer from getting through?

When we understand how God's kingdom and satan's kingdom each work, we're better prepared to remain steadfast in faith, staying the course until we receive the answer. We also recognize the need to engage in spiritual warfare to receive the answer, and more quickly.

When Jesus was crucified and then resurrected, He gained victory over satan. Just before Jesus ascended into Heaven, He gave His followers that same power and authority over satan (Luke 10:19) so we could use those weapons to be victorious.

Satan has no authority or power over you unless you agree with him.

Ask any military strategist or commander, and they'll say the best way to defeat the enemy is to understand the adversary's weaknesses, strengths, and limitations and then take the offensive.

Spiritual warfare is no different.

To win our battles over satan, we must

- understand his character, tactics, and limitations,
- understand the weapons of warfare we have from God, and
- understand how to use those weapons most effectively against him and his forces.

The name of Jesus is superior in power and ultimate authority.

There is no greater power than the name of Jesus. No less than twenty-three Scripture verses declare the power of His name.

The Story of Living in a Haunted House

As a young father, I led our family into what we believed was our dream home in sunny Southern California. The property was massive: a 5,200-square-foot house perched on a hill with surrounding acreage and a panoramic 360-degree view.

The home had been in probate for over a year, untouched by potential buyers. So we took the opportunity to buy the property for a fraction of its million-dollar value. We saw it as a blessing from the Lord, unaware of the eerie events that awaited us.

We had learned the house's dark history; a murder-suicide had occurred inside. To us, though, the house seemed more of a blessing than anything malevolent.

As the months passed, we realized we were living in a spiritual battleground—not simply bad luck or creepy crawlies. Soon after we'd moved in, events took a strange turn, beginning with little things. Bugs.

One night at bedtime, while playing my guitar and singing to my young daughter, Kara, she noticed something black moving across the opposite wall. I turned on the light, and we were startled to find a five-inch poisonous scorpion. Kara calmly commented, "Oh, Daddy, don't worry; I see those in the house all the time."

What appeared the next evening was more unsettling. Paula was reading her Bible when a six-inch centipede fell from the ceiling onto her head.

Centipedes and scorpions became a continual plague with new ones showing up every day and throughout the house. I chalked up the bugs to the natural environment surrounding the residence, unaware that these disturbances were signs of something far more sinister.

Then the voices. . . . Those were harder to ignore.

Paula frequently heard someone calling her within the house when no one else was home. She said the voices were unmistakably familiar as if one of our children needed her. But they weren't there. The eerie callouts grew louder, more persistent, and had an unnatural, disturbing quality.

Then Kara, and even visiting friends, experienced similarly strange phenomena—familiar voices of people not there.

Our son's friend was visiting when late one evening after dark, the friend saw something terrifying through the window. He claimed he had seen someone dragging a body down the driveway and into the brush. A search of the area revealed no body nor anyone around the house. Yet he was so shaken by what he swore he'd seen, he left the house quickly and never again returned.

Despite the alarming incidents, my thoughts gave way to logical explanations. As a practical businessman and professional pilot, I hesitated to link the disturbing events to something supernatural.

The turning point came when Kara experienced one of her most frightening encounters. She was watching TV when she heard her mother's voice calling. "Kara, come here for a minute."

She didn't think much of it until she remembered she was home alone. Panic surged through her. Then the once familiar voice grew sinister, morphing into a raspy, guttural sound, repeating over and over, "Kara! Come here for a minute!"

In intense fear, Kara ran from the house to a friend's home nearby.

Another evening, Paula was home alone when she heard what sounded like me clearing my throat directly behind her. She said the sound was close and unmistakably my voice. Terror hit when she remembered I was thousands of miles away in another country.

I'd had enough; *This has become personal!*

The frightening moments were piling up. Paula and I looked back at that time and recognized we had been slow to take action, not fully grasping the severity of what was happening. We were young and untrained in spiritual warfare, and no one we knew had experienced anything similar. Back then, few people talked about hauntings or supernatural activity.

We hadn't realized the house had come with more than a great price; it carried a dark, sinister past expressing itself in the present.

Another incident occurred with Kara. She had a brass bed that squeaked when anyone moved on it. Our dog, Wicket, a Lhasa Apso, often slept on the foot of her bed, and when he'd scratch his ears, the bed would creak.

One night, Kara felt that familiar movement and heard the bed squeak. She kicked Wicket off with her foot, only to feel him back on her bed again. When the movement and noise repeated, she kicked him off a second time and got up to carry him out of her room. She turned on the lights to realize Wicket wasn't even in the room. What had she kicked off her bed—twice? Searching, she found Wicket in her brother's room, where the dog had been the entire time.

At that point, our family jointly discussed all the individual events. We realized we had each dealt independently with bizarre occurrences, unaware of the combined magnitude.

Immediately after our discussion, the disturbing activity grew worse—fast. The increase was as if our mutual acknowledgment had agitated and somehow empowered the sinister forces threatening our family.

At the time, I had little experience with demonic warfare. And I didn't believe most stories about the subject. From my analytical background, my logical mind kept telling me, *These occurrences can't be real.* Yet they were happening to each of us—even to me.

In that era, there was no internet or easy search for answers. I could have searched by other means, and I should have. But I delayed.

That was a mistake.

One Sunday after church, we returned home to find all the doors and windows wide open. Immediately suspecting a break-in, I called the police.

The officers searched the entire house while we waited in suspense on the driveway.

They found nothing—no intruders, no signs of forced entry, and nothing stolen. Yet *every* door and *every* window were open. It made no sense . . . , again.

The paranormal activity intensified.

Our son, Eric, had another friend, Kyle, over one evening. They were in his room when they heard a bloodcurdling scream, and someone shouted Kyle's name. The scream was so loud it woke Paula and me, and we rushed to check on the boys.

Eric and Kyle were visibly shaken. Kyle flat-out refused to stay in the house. Who could blame him? I drove him home.

Days later, I was awakened in the night by loud, eerie noises, sounding like an intruder in the house. Convinced there was a trespasser, I armed myself and searched room by room. I found nothing.

That does it!

I had finally accepted that even though nothing was logical about the occurrences, they were real, and they were demonic.

Those truths pushed me deeper into my Bible. *How does Jesus deal with demons?* I searched and devoured what Jesus taught about fighting and winning against this invisible evil enemy.

The "intruder" disturbance had marked a turning point in me. I had accepted that our house was haunted and that the murder-suicide history had left a dark spiritual presence that was tormenting us. It was time—long overdue—to take a stand. I couldn't believe I'd waited this long.

Desperate for answers, I sought a seasoned expert in spiritual warfare. He wasn't just knowledgeable; he was battle-tested. His wisdom, drawn from years of experience detailed in the books he'd written, became a lifeline in our fight.

We soon learned why the house had remained unsold for so long. I had befriended a local realtor who had heard many things about the house's history. Not only did the house have a dark legacy of murder and suicide, but also satanic rituals. He shared that neighbors had seen strange, ritualistic-type gatherings that appeared to be sinister ceremonies.

Although we had bought a house with knowledge of the tragic past, we hadn't known that forces from hell had been invited and stayed. We needed to cleanse our home of everything possibly linked to the dark forces at work.

We sat down as a family, and Paula and I asked our children to join us in getting rid of anything that could be a conduit inviting evil into our lives. Although we had not initiated the problem, we wanted to ensure we were in no way enabling it.

The night after our family meeting, I had a vivid dream. I was surrounded by snakes—huge serpents everywhere. I began cutting off their heads with a machete. But the more I attacked them, the more they multiplied. In my dream, what eventually destroyed the snakes was fire.

I woke up convinced that the dream was a message from God, directing us to burn up everything that could serve as an invitation to the evil in our house.

We gathered everything we believed could be a demonic conduit—posters, records, statues, and artifacts from our many trips to other countries. We prepared to burn them all.

Incinerating the items wasn't just about getting rid of potential conduits; the action represented a spiritual purge.

Everything we'd gathered, we placed in a large burn barrel in the yard and set the items on fire. As the fire did its work, the smell became unbearable—an odor I can only describe as burning hair and death permeating the air.

Together, Paula and I anointed the inside of the house with oil, praying over every opening—doors and windows. We commanded the spirits of darkness to "get out, in Jesus's name!"

As we worked from back to front, ending in the living room, Eric and Kara alerted us to a strange, dense, green smoke-like fog about a foot thick, moving along the ceiling. They had discovered the mass when looking in the large mirror above our fireplace. Also eerie, the foggy green substance could only be seen in the mirror as the reflection it cast. It flowed from the back of the house toward the front door and out, moving ahead of where Paula and I were anointing the doors and windows while praying. This continued for about two hours.

When we finished anointing the front entrance, the smoky matter disappeared, and we knew the evil presence had departed. It was gone.

Immediately, the atmosphere in our home changed. The house felt different—peaceful.

We had reclaimed our home by taking spiritual authority, speaking aloud the Word of God, and commanding the evil spirits to leave in the name of Jesus.

The house's haunted history of murder and suicide had indeed been a site of satanic rituals.

Looking back, I see how unprepared I was for that spiritual battle. Yet the process taught us invaluable lessons about the demonic, our need for vigilance, the power of prayer, and the power of taking authority in Jesus's name. What had started as a nightmare became a testimony to the strength of *believing* God's Word and *acting* in faith by speaking to evil with authority: "Get out! Be gone, in the name of Jesus!"

The house that had once terrified us became a testament to the power of the name of Jesus and the supernatural force of atomic faith that conquers evil.

That haunted house was far more than a creepy place; it was a battleground, a war zone of spiritual conflict. Yet through it all, our family emerged stronger—more spiritually aware and better equipped to take authority over evil. We learned how to stand firm, armed with faith and the power and authority of God.

The Takeaway

Evil spirits (demons) can only enter where access is granted. Satanic ceremonies—even those in the name of fun or entertainment—open doorways between the physical and demonic realms, granting spiritual entry and authority to evil entities.

Once inside, they try to expand their reach to humans, especially children—their ultimate prize and easiest target.

Demons are disembodied spirits who prefer to be in physical bodies to further express their evil character through human hosts (Matthew 12:43; Luke 11:24).

Demons are disembodied spirits.

Evil spirits operate where they have permissible authority. For example, a ritual can grant access to a location. A curse placed on an object can attach a demon. Evil or traumatic events can create pathways that allow demons to access people and places. Evil spirits can then remain until cast out by the greater power—the only authority that exceeds all evil forces: the name of Jesus (Philippians 2:9).

What satan intended for evil in our haunted house, God transformed for His glory and our good. He shows no favoritism. What Jesus has done for us, He will do for you.

Do Not Fear Demons or Satan

Satan is the original con man, always trying to trick us into giving up whatever God has given us. Demons use deception to gain ground wherever we allow in our lives.

Evil is often packaged to seem harmless, such as participating in a séance for fun, reading science fiction centered on dark forces, getting a tarot card reading, watching sinister movies, or listening to music laced with darkness. But even the smallest foothold can be an entry point. From a seemingly insignificant choice, these forces push to expand their influence through subtle manipulation and temptation—disguised as innocent distractions.

Satan's kingdom is currently here on Earth, operating through this world's system. The Bible tells us his limited authority here is temporary. Although we live in satan's kingdom by default, when we're reborn spiritually (by faith in Jesus), our citizenship transfers to God's kingdom, with rights and benefits provided to us through Jesus.

Satan has always wanted God's glory. He hates humankind because every person is created in God's image and with the potential for salvation, which he can never obtain.

When you become a child of God through your belief in Jesus Christ as your Savior, you become a primary enemy of satan. He is aware of the power and authority Jesus has made available to you, and he works endlessly to rob you of your authority through deception, false teaching, and lack of knowledge.

The Bible has alerted us to this danger: "My people are destroyed for lack of knowledge" (Hosea 4:6).

Checklist: Authority Over Demonic Forces

✓ Be diligent—to believe God's written Word.

✓ Be diligent—to establish your belief in His Word.

✓ Be diligent—to take action by faith based upon what you believe.

✓ Be diligent—to replace satan's lies with what is true.

✓ Be diligent—to repeatedly speak out loud God's written promises that pertain to your need.

Agreeing with the written Word is always God's will for you.

Victory is yours as you keep Jesus Christ and the Word of God in first place in your life.

> The weapons of our warfare are not carnal but mighty in God for pulling down strongholds, casting down arguments and every high thing that exalts itself against the knowledge of God, bringing every thought into captivity to the obedience of Christ.
> — 2 Corinthians 10:4–5

Each day we face an invisible enemy whose purpose is to steal, kill, and destroy. However, you can overcome the unseen enemy by

- putting your faith in God,
- standing on the truth of His Word, and
- wielding the spiritual weapons He has provided.

Satan flees and demons recoil when the name of Jesus is spoken with faith and authority.

Chapter 7

PRAYING FOR YOUR LOVED ONES
THE MIRACULOUS JOEL GREEN STORY

I exhort first of all that supplications,
prayers, intercessions, and giving of thanks
be made for all men. . . . For this is good
and acceptable in the sight of God our
Savior, who desires all men to be saved and
to come to the knowledge of the truth.
— 1 Timothy 2:1, 3–4

PEOPLE OFTEN FEEL DISCOURAGED WHEN THEIR PRAYERS FOR SOMEONE THEY LOVE SEEM TO GO UNANSWERED. They may start to wonder if God is even listening. But when we learn to pray the way Jesus taught, everything changes. Our prayers become stronger, more effective, and full of power. They begin to bring real miracles—transforming lives—and can even change the world.

When praying for others, there are two essentials to keep in mind:

- Love requires freedom. God will not violate a person's free will.
- No one wants their free will taken away or ignored. When people feel their freedom of choice threatened, they often resist and push back.

Many people pray for others without clear direction—like firing a shotgun without training and hoping to hit a target. This usually occurs because they're missing some key elements and haven't received the training needed to pray in a way that brings results. Sadly, this is one reason why even devoted believers can spend years praying for their loved ones and still see little or no change.

Let's consider how most people pray for others. Something like this: "Oh God, Jennifer needs to get right with You. Please help her get saved and find the truth."

Sometimes they go further, listing their loved one's mistakes or sins: "Lord, Jennifer is using drugs again. She's been bailed out before. But now, God, You've got to save her, or I don't know what we'll do."

The fact is, God already knows what's happening with Jennifer and what she needs. He wants her to repent of her sins, believe in Jesus as her Savior, and fully rely on Him. So why do these prayers usually remain unanswered?

Such prayers are certainly full of love and concern. But are those prayers engaged in how Jesus taught us to fight in spiritual warfare? Let's break this down and learn how to pray effectively, once and for all.

I've heard a lot of prayers that sound like this: "Jennifer won't listen to me. She's not open to the gospel or to what Jesus taught. The more I try to talk to her about God, the less she wants to talk to me."

The ineffectiveness of such prayers is that we're trying to bring our loved ones closer to God through human methods instead of *using the spiritual power tools* Jesus taught. Rather than depending on God's power, we often rely on mental and emotional pressure. That method will never have the same impact on a person's heart as the power from Heaven. Where is the *faith* in prayers like the one above? There is none. Most people don't fully understand how Jesus taught us to pray nor how to use His spiritual weapons.

Moreover, we forget about the spiritual battle that's constantly underway between satan and our loved ones. Many followers of Jesus don't realize that people who haven't been spiritually reborn are blind and deaf to God's truth. The Bible tells us that "the message of the cross is foolishness to those who are perishing" (1 Corinthians 1:18).

People praying for their loved ones often don't understand what's happening in the spiritual realm. When their prayers continue unanswered, they start losing hope and faith. Eventually, they give up praying altogether, not understanding why their prayers were ineffective.

If we want to bring God's power into our lives here on Earth, we must use every spiritual weapon Jesus taught and use them correctly. These weapons are far more potent than any tactics satan uses.

When we pray "in Jesus's name" and use the other weapons and tools He has provided, we can break through satan's lies and traps that keep our loved ones from seeing and hearing the truth.

There are several vital principles to understand when praying for your loved ones. Before diving into those, consider the following true story (recounted from my book *Flight To Heaven*) that shows how God powerfully revealed His faithfulness to prayer.

The Miraculous Joel Green Story

My left shoulder rapidly deteriorated in the months after the plane crash, making another surgery unavoidable. My doctor had one available date and insisted the surgery was essential. Looking back, I realize God chose that date for a greater purpose.

I vowed the surgery would be my last—a promise I now laugh about, having made that pledge before each of the seventeen surgeries since surviving the fatal crash.

On the scheduled day, the familiar staff at St. Joseph's Hospital in Burbank, California, greeted me warmly. Some recognized me as a frequent patient, and others remembered me from my brief "fifteen minutes of fame" on local news. They were kind and eager to assist with my recovery.

While I was grateful for their hospitality, the hospital itself felt like a prison of pain, tied to the many difficult surgeries that had kept me there and returning for months.

Entering my assigned room, I noticed the drawn curtain separating me from my roommate. Moments later, an angry voice yelled from that direction, "Nurse! Get in here! Can't you do anything right? Get in here now!"

When the nurse bustled in, I saw the weariness and frustration on her face from dealing with such demeaning and demanding treatment.

My roommate rattled off a list of his complaints to her: nothing was right—the food was terrible, the TV was on the wrong channel, the remote control was intermittent, and the volume wouldn't adjust. The man was utterly miserable and seeping with anger that poured out when anyone attended to him.

Wow, I'm going to have to put up with this guy all night?

I considered requesting a room change, but a gentle nudge from God's Spirit directed me to think further about the angry man. *What put him in the hospital? What has his life been like? Where is he regarding a relationship with God?*

Suddenly, an overwhelming, deep love for the old man washed over me with a strong urge to talk with him. *God, what could I possibly say to him? Give me the words and Your strength and patience to speak as Jesus would.*

The urging within me grew stronger, so I maneuvered out of bed and gingerly let go of the rail. I had come into the hospital by wheelchair due to the full cast on my left leg and one arm strapped to my stomach.

I hopped on one foot to the curtain, gave it a wiggle, and tentatively said, "Sir? . . . Hello. I'm your roommate, Dale. What's your name, sir?"

No response.

An eternity ticked by before I heard his bristled tone of irritation. "The name's Green. Joel Green."

"Well, sir, . . . looks like we'll be sharing this room tonight," I said through the drapery. "It's nice to meet you."

I was about to return to bed when he yanked back the curtain, startling me. His eyes glared at me from his leathery, weathered face that quickly changed to surprise. "You're just a kid!" He looked me up and down, taking in all my physical constraints. "What are you in here for?" he asked as though there couldn't possibly be anything more my body required.

I chuckled and explained, "Well, sir, I'm the only survivor of the plane that crashed into the aviation mausoleum—back in July."

His features shifted with recall. "I heard about that on the news." I was now the one surprised. He scratched at his worn, stubbled cheek, his eyes fixed on the ceiling, mouth downturned in thought. "'Cruel Irony?' or something . . . ," vaguely remembering one of the headlines.

I was impressed. The newspaper headline had read, "Fate? Coincidence? Or Cruel Irony?"

We talked about the crash and the irony of smashing into a mausoleum erected to honor dead aviators. I shared the miracle of my survival.

The love of Jesus for this man had filled me, and I could no longer hold back the question pressing in me. "Mr. Green, do you know Jesus Christ? He's the only reason I'm alive," I quickly offered. "He lives in me now. He's given me joy, peace, and purpose I'd never known before."

The man stared at me, at a loss for words by the abrupt change of topic and my streaming testimony. I plowed forward. "Mr. Green, Jesus died for you. Do you know Him as your Savior?"

He looked away and stared out the large paned window, silent.

God's love for the man was immense, pouring from my heart. "Mr. Green, Jesus Christ loves you and provided the free gift of salvation—for you. The Bible says God didn't send His Son into the world to condemn the world but that through Him the world might be saved."

I hopped nearer. "Sir? Have you heard about this gift of salvation through Jesus, God's Son?" Mr. Green remained still, but his expression contorted, and tears formed in his ruddy eyes.

Finally, he spoke, turning his head and looking directly at me. "Dale, I'm the son of a preacher." He'd lost the gruff edge of his tone, his voice now shaky. "I'm seventy-seven years old, kid, and I've been running from God most all my life." He took the tissue I handed him and swiped his eyes. "I've waited too long. Why would God want me now?" His sigh released a heavy sadness.

"Oh, Mr. Green, no, sir. I'm sorry to disagree, but it's never too late. The Bible says God's timing is *now*. Sir, why not let go of any past mistakes? When God forgives, He forgets. He said He throws our sins away as far as the east is from the west. I don't fully understand it, but I know it's true 'cause it happened to me."

The old man had turned his face back to the window and didn't respond.

"Mr. Green, give God your life now, and I promise you'll never regret it."

Silence.

Had I been too bold? Too pushy? Although I was worried about his reaction, the love in my heart was uncontainable and overriding, just as it had been after I woke from my three-day coma—a flood of love for all of humanity, unlike I'd ever experienced before the crash.

A lot was at stake for Mr. Green—everything. Softly I asked, "Mr. Green? Would you be willing to pray to God right now? We can ask Him together for forgiveness."

No response. Then he whispered, "Yeah, I . . . I'd like that."

He didn't seem to know what to say next, and, truthfully, I was just as uncertain. I was a young pilot, a college student, a crash survivor . . . not experienced in telling people about Jesus. But I remembered God's promise to provide the words whenever I needed them.

"Just say this prayer after me, Mr. Green." He nodded, and I took a deep breath and reached out in invitation to take my hand. He opened his fist and took hold of my hand, and I began to pray. "Dear God—"

"Dear God," he followed.

"I'm sorry I've been running away from You. I should have been running to You."

He repeated the admission with quiet humility.

"Lord, forgive me of my sins. I'm tired of running from You."

As soon as those words left his lips, he broke down, sobbing. My tears also took course, and I squeezed his rough, leathery hand. After a pause, I resumed, "Dear Father—"

"Dear Father," he said, gripping my hand tighter.

"Thank You for Your unending love." I paused as he spoke the same. "Thank You for sending Your Son to die on the cross for me. Jesus, I invite You into my heart and life right now. Please take control of my life. Thank You, God. Amen."

He firmly squeezed my hand, dried his tears, and thanked me.

We talked until the nurse returned to check on him. His attitude with her reflected a changed, humbled man.

She noticed and gave me a wink and a smile. Mr. Green was now polite, gentle, and kind.

After she left, he said, "Call me Joel."

We talked into the night and became genuine friends. He spoke at length about his parents and their tireless prayers for him throughout his teens and all the years beyond. They'd never given up.

Though his father had passed into Heaven, his mother was still alive and in her final sunset years. He couldn't wait to tell her he'd at last stopped running from God.

He and I had bonded in our brief span of confinement together. We were buddies and spiritual brothers. Anyone who puts their faith in Jesus Christ as their Savior instantly becomes part of God's huge kingdom family.

Bright and early the following day, while I was being prepped for surgery, Joel's side of the room was quiet.

As I was wheeled out, the last thing I remembered was that the nurse had injected something into my hip. In response, I said what had become my hospital hallmark—a bit of a joke among the small group of familiar staff. "Carol, did I tell you this is my last surgery?" She chuckled, her smile blurring as I drifted off.

—

"Wake up, Dale. . . . Wake up." Someone was tapping my cheek, coaxing me back into consciousness.

When I gained focus, I was staring into the face of Dr. Graham, looming over me with an excited smile. "Dale, . . . I can hardly believe it! There was no deterioration in your shoulder muscles! At all!" He straightened, confident from my wide eyes that I'd heard him. "I only had to shorten a few muscles and ligaments. They were much healthier than I could've hoped for."

Usually calm and professional, Dr. Grahm couldn't contain his excitement. He blurted, "I believe that one day you might be able to lift your arm to forty-five degrees. That would be amazing considering that sixty percent of the muscles and ligaments were removed and the bone restructuring we did!"

"No, Dr. Graham." I slowly shook my head, a lazy roll back and forth against the pillow. "Thanks, doc, . . . but God will restore my shoulder—and one day, I'll be able to lift my arm over my head! Just wait. You'll see."

As a couple of hospital attendants guided my gurney through a maze of corridors to my room, I marveled at the wondrous God I was serving. The list of miracles and answered prayers just kept increasing.

After I was settled onto my bed, I looked over to say hello to Joel, but his bed was empty. I asked the nurse, motioning with my good arm, "Hey, where's my buddy, Joel?"

Nurse Carol subtly shook her head and said, "He's gone, Dale. I'm so sorry. Joel passed away while you were in surgery."

My breath left me, and my mind went blank. I felt as though my heart had stopped. I was confused. Then a thought hit me. *Joel is in Heaven! Joel made it home!* The sadness left as suddenly as it had knocked the breath from me. *He made it home. He's with Jesus.* I would see him again.

A Scripture sprang to mind: "The Lord is not slack concerning His promise, as some count slackness, but is longsuffering toward us, not willing that any should perish but that all should come to repentance" (2 Peter 3:9).

Right then, I vowed to never again be timid about sharing the good news of Jesus Christ. I realized my hospital stay was only partly about my shoulder and God's healing plan. It had also been about Joel's spiritual birth and his finding eternal life in Jesus.

Salvation hadn't been too late for Joel after all. God had answered his mother's and father's longstanding prayers.

Praying for Your Loved One's Salvation

Let's explore more ways to strengthen our prayers—more power tools that will change everything. Such breakthrough goes beyond what we can do on our own, so using all of God's atomic tools is critical to bind satan from holding our loved ones from the truth.

Once we realize that the devil—not your loved one— is the real problem, the first step in prayer is clear: Get the devil out of their way so they can be free to hear, see, understand, and receive the truth from God.

Jesus confronted us with logic when he asked, "How can one enter a strong man's house and plunder his goods, unless he first binds the strong man?" (Matthew 12:29).

1. **Speak Directly with Bold Confidence**

Speak directly, boldly, and confidently to the evil spirit deceiving your loved one. Example:

> *You evil spirit deceiving Jennifer, blinding her from the truth of God and the gospel message, I bind you in Jesus's name! I curse your efforts against Jennifer and pull down the deception from over her. I claim that Jennifer is free to choose eternal life in Jesus!*
>
> *I command the spiritual scales over Jennifer's eyes to fall off and the confusion and resistance in Jennifer's mind to be gone in Jesus's name!*
>
> *Father, I ask that Jennifer would recognize her need for a Savior and that she would give her heart to the Lord Jesus.*

If you speak directly and commandingly to evil in the name of Jesus and you pray with atomic faith to the Father (like the above), believing it is *done* in your loved one as it is in Heaven, you are

- taking *authority over* the enemy,
- casting out evil spirits that have been deceiving and trapping your loved one, and
- bringing God's will and power into the situation.

Remember, the enemy never stops trying to take control. You're in a spiritual tug-of-war. Your declarations are not one and done; the demons you've cast out *will* constantly tempt your loved one to let them back in. That's why it's crucial to "pray without ceasing" (1 Thessalonians 5:16) and pray with the authority of Jesus for your loved one.

Your prayers don't need to be long; they need to be powerful, backed by the authority of God's Word.

2. **See Yourself As God Sees You: An Extension of Jesus**

When you pray for a person's salvation, you're a laborer in the spiritual harvest. Remember, God works *through* His people.

> Jesus looked out at the multitudes and said to His disciples, "The harvest truly is plentiful, but the laborers are few. Therefore pray the Lord of the harvest to send out laborers into His harvest."
> — Matthew 9:37–38

3. **Be Persistent in Hope, Belief, and Faith**

We know God's will is for *all* people to receive Jesus, and we know that if we're praying in agreement with Him, He hears and answers. As an intercessory prayer warrior, you must use the *hope, belief,* and *faith* you've read about throughout this book, as presented from God's Word, and persistently pray *until the answer becomes visible.*

Remember God's message to me about the man lost in the Grand Canyon? "Don't stop until he's found." Don't stop your persistence in hope, belief, and atomic faith until your loved one is found in Jesus, in humble repentance, faith, and surrender to Him as Lord over their hearts and lives.

In the meantime, remember that defeating satan is a powerful one-two punch. After your persistent prayers of atomic faith have removed the spiritual blinders and deceptions from your loved one, you must continue to persistently pray and speak your atomic faith, declaring aloud, as fact, "My loved one *is* being saved in Jesus's name!"

4. **Ask for Reinforcements**

Ask God to send other followers of Jesus into your loved one's life, people who will witness to them, plant the seeds of God's Word, and be persistent in prayer with atomic faith. Example:

Father, I'm asking You to send laborers into Jennifer's life. Send those who will plant spiritual seeds to help Jennifer hear, see, and receive the truth from God.

5. **Praise, Worship, and Thank God**

Praising, worshipping, and thanking Jesus for the victorious outcome—before it's visible—are atomic acts of faith that release strength into the spiritual battle. When we praise, worship, and thank God, we're using these additional tools as actions of faith that break strongholds.

Powerful Prayer Promises

This is the confidence that we have in Him, that if we ask anything according to His will, He hears us. And if we know that He hears us, whatever we ask, we know that we have the petitions that we have asked of Him. — 1 John 5:14–15

Let us not grow weary while doing good, for in due season we shall reap if we do not lose heart. — Galatians 6:9

The miracle of Mr. Green is an example of what causes Heaven to rejoice. Joel is home in Heaven now. His parents' prayers were answered in the final hours before Joel's earthly life ended. They persisted in prayer until the answer came.

Never stop praying for those you love. Keep asking God to send the right people into their lives so they may find eternal life in Jesus.

"There is joy in the presence of the angels of God over one sinner who repents." — Luke 15:10

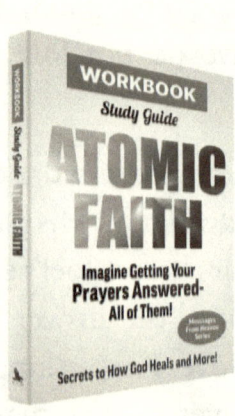

Chapter 8

PRAISE YOUR WAY INTO BREAKTHROUGH
THE NOLAN REED STORY

God inhabits the praises of His people.
— Psalm 22:3

FAITH ISN'T JUST SOMETHING YOU HAVE—IT'S SOMETHING YOU USE. To see real results in your prayers, you must understand every facet of faith and wield each one with precision. A secret weapon is *praise*. Praising Jesus doesn't just strengthen your faith; praising fuels it.

> For whatever is born of God overcomes the world. And this is the victory that has overcome the world— our faith. — 1 John 5:4

Are you praying for a loved one? Believing for healing? Longing to reclaim something precious that was lost?

Whatever your battle, faith isn't a feeling—it's a force. And when you wield faith with full confidence and precision, breakthrough comes faster than you ever imagined.

The Action of Seeking

Matthew 6:33 begins with the directive to "Seek first the kingdom of God"—an action, as we saw in Chapter 3. We can't seek anything by sitting still and simply hoping or believing. Seeking ignites our faith because seeking requires action. Faith is acting on what we believe.

You may be wondering, *What is the "kingdom of God"?* God's kingdom is the spiritual realm where His authority reigns. His kingdom includes Himself—God, Jesus, and the Holy Spirit—and spiritual beings such as angels and people who have been spiritually reborn.

We learned that the second part of the verse presents a specific outcome as a promise for obeying Jesus's directive: "These things shall be added to you."

What things? The things you're believing and praying for.

When you submit to God and seek His will *before* making your request, that prioritizing will cause you to pray in agreement with Him. When you pray in agreement with God's will, you have *confidence* that He hears your prayers and will answer (1 John 5:14).

Seek God's will before you pray, so your prayer agrees with God.

Natural vs. Spiritual

Within God's kingdom are two dimensions: the natural and spiritual realms. The two intersect and interact in response to God's plan, our prayers, and our faith.

If we're connected to God through a relationship with Jesus, we're *within* His kingdom and have access to both the natural and spiritual dimensions. We've been given the authority of Jesus to use His superior spiritual power (Ephesians 1:19–21).

Satan and his demons are subject to the name of Jesus— and to us, the followers of Jesus, if we use His name with understanding and submission to everything His name represents.

Righteous Authority

The second directive in Matthew 6:33 is to seek God's *righteousness*. What does that mean? Choosing to place ourselves under the authority of Jesus.

Although we strive to walk worthy of our salvation, we can never be perfect enough for a holy God. Anything or anyone less than absolute perfection is unacceptable to Him because He is pure holiness. Yet due to God's abundant love for humankind, He provided a perfect and spotless sacrifice to take our place and provide a holy covering for our imperfections.

How to Seek God's Righteousness

When we repent of sin and invite Jesus into our lives, we are reborn spiritually—Jesus's righteousness replaces our sin. His perfection makes those who trust in Him acceptable before a holy God.

In New Testament teachings, "righteous" signifies a state of being in right relationship with God through faith in Jesus Christ. As we seek to know Jesus better, live to please Him more, and walk in agreement with His Word, we are seeking His righteousness. Our right standing also gives us access to Jesus's power and other benefits—the abundant life Jesus promised.

Jesus reveals both satan's agenda for us and God's desire for us in John 10:10: "The thief does not come except to steal, and to kill, and to destroy. I have come that they may have life, and that they may have it more abundantly."

Seeking the kingdom of God and seeking His righteousness are intentional, decisive actions on our part. Seeking is not simply believing that God's kingdom and His righteousness exist. No. We must take action to *seek* to align our will with God's.

Praise is another form of Heaven's power we can bring to Earth that changes satan's destruction into God's abundant life. The following story is about releasing the power of praise in faith to bring about breakthrough.

The Nolan Reed Story

In the early 1980s, I found myself seated in the third row of a packed ministers' conference in a large US city. The auditorium buzzed with energy as over five thousand attendees filled the space. The event was hosted and organized by Dr. Charles, a minister I had flown as pilot on several occasions through our aviation company. Paula and I had long been supporting his ministry.

Nolan Reed, a man in his late thirties, was introduced as a speaker. We learned that through Nolan's ministry, teams traveled to various countries to preach the gospel of Jesus, distribute food and clothing, and supply Bibles.

Nolan shared a personal, heart-wrenching story. While on a mission in Russia, he received a telegram from home in the US informing him that his wife of fifteen years had died in a fatal car crash.

In the moments following the shocking news, Nolan also experienced an intense wave of anger—directed at God. Being in Russia, he couldn't easily or quickly return to the US, and communication was limited.

When he finally arrived home, his worst fears were confirmed. His life had turned upside down.

Two years passed as Nolan struggled to pick up the pieces of his life. He had five children to care for and a successful organization to run. Struggling with grief, he slipped into deep depression. He could barely work, and reading his Bible or praying was difficult.

As I listened to Nolan recount his story two years since losing his wife, it was clear that his pain was still agonizingly fresh. Although he knew his wife was safely home in Heaven, he continued to feel the intense loss.

Then he shared the pivotal moment that triggered his breakthrough. He had received a phone call from his mentor, Dr. Charles, inviting him to a personal meeting. During the scheduled conversation, Dr. Charles asked Nolan how he was coping with the loss. Nolan opened up about his deep depression and how he couldn't seem to move forward.

In response, Charles told of his past grief in losing two of his children in two unrelated accidents. He shared the immense pain he and his wife endured and what the Spirit of God taught him that helped him move beyond the debilitating and paralyzing emotions.

Nolan listened intently, relating to the shock and grief of enormous loss. He reluctantly admitted that his depression had reached a severe, all-consuming level. He confessed that he was angry at God for allowing such a horrible thing to occur, especially since he had been serving God at the time. He admitted he was confused and struggling to even sense God's presence.

In frustration, he asked Charles, "Why would a loving God allow such a senseless accident to happen?" His wife had been killed by a driver who had run a red light. She had done nothing wrong.

Nolan acknowledged that despite knowing he should move past the anger, he just couldn't. He was furious about how she had died, and he felt incapacitated. The other driver was barely injured. Nolan couldn't shake the bitterness over how unfair it all was.

Dr. Charles said he understood. He acknowledged that he and his wife had been stuck for a time in self-pity. He described the feeling as a self-centered sorrow and pity regarding their suffering. He affirmed that grieving is normal, a natural response to tragedy, but that grieving can easily slip into depression, which is something entirely different.

He put his hand on Nolan's shoulder. "Listen to me, son. You must praise God to get through this. You have to praise Him!" He shared more of what God had taught him. "When I lost my children, I went through a similar experience each time. It was terrible. But God showed me that nothing would change until I acted in faith and praised Him, regardless of the circumstances and how I felt.

"You won't feel like praising God," Dr. Charles reiterated. "Nothing in you wants to praise. But you must do it. Praise Him by faith, Nolan. You truly have no other option if you want to break through the depression. It's a choice, not a feeling. A choice to choose God's way in this situation."

He explained, "Right now, satan has you entangled in his trap. You're caught. But God has provided a way for you to set yourself free."

"You're right," Nolan responded, "I do have a choice and I don't want to praise God. That doesn't feel like an option right now."

Dr. Charles persisted. "Nolan, just lift your hands and simply say, 'Praise God.' Do it right now," he urged.

Their eyes locked in silent conflict, and Nolan said, "I told you, I *can't*."

"Can't or won't?"

"I *can't*," Nolan insisted.

"I think you won't," Dr. Charles responded. Again, he urged Nolan, "Just lift your hands and say, 'Lord, I praise you. God, I don't hold you responsible for this. I praise you, Lord. You are worthy of praise, no matter what's happened. Right now, I give You honor and praise.'"

Nolan listened, but he couldn't bring himself to praise.

Charles was honest, based on his freeing experience of praise. "Nolan, you won't get anywhere if you stay in this position. As long as you refuse to budge, satan will make things worse. You'll feel sorrier for yourself and stay blinded from seeing the good in your life." With more urgency, he added, "Don't let satan win this, Nolan! You're better than that!

"You have five wonderful children and hundreds of people who love and support you. I was at the funeral, Nolan. I saw the outpouring of love." He painted the picture of truth. "You have a fruitful ministry. This isn't the end of your life!" he charged. "You must praise God for who He is and what He's done for you."

When they parted, Nolan felt challenged to take action, yet he still felt he couldn't act on his mentor's advice.

The next morning, Nolan sensed the Holy Spirit stirring in him, reminding him of Dr. Charles's words.

The conference arena was silent. We were all listening intently. "I saw in the mirror how far I'd let myself go," he continued. "I looked terrible and felt empty—a shell of the man I used to be, having spent more than a year in deep, debilitating depression. Staring at my reflection, I stated, 'This has to change.'"

"I lifted my arms just a little"—he demonstrated, his hands barely at ear level—"and with no emotion or conviction, I muttered, 'Praise the Lord.' But nothing seemed to change. It was a start, a seed of faith."

For the first time since receiving the news of his wife's death, Nolan had spoken three words that took a stand of faith in the battle against depression and self-pity.

"I lifted my hands again and spoke a little louder: 'Praise the Lord.' And I did it again and again."

As he recounted the story, he looked down, clearly reliving those difficult moments. Even though his experiences were painful, we could each relate in some way. All five thousand of us had experienced some form of wilderness, as all people do—maybe not the sudden, tragic death of a spouse or children, but something that shook us deeply to our core.

"As I stood in front of the mirror, forcing my hands higher, I pushed myself to speak louder. Dozens of times I spoke words of praise: 'Praise the Lord. Thank You, God. Praise You, Jesus.'"

He admitted, "I'd like to say that the breakthrough came at that moment, and everything was fine from then on. But that wasn't the case.

"The next morning, I stood in front of the mirror again, lifted my hands even higher, and spoke the same words of praise louder. I looked at my reflection and said, 'Praise the Lord. Praise God.' Then I said, 'Praise You, Jesus,' and I kept going until something inside me took over, as though I wasn't alone in praising.

"As I kept praising—not because I felt like it but because I was choosing to praise in faith—the burden loosened. I continued until the anger, grief, and depression lightened more and more until finally, after carrying that weight for so long, the heaviness lifted. It was gone, and a tiny seed of faith had taken root."

Nolan shared that one week after meeting with Dr. Charles and spending the week in praise, he looked in the mirror and realized he was looking at a very different man.

"Praising God has brought me peace. I have joy in my heart that I thought I'd never experience again!

"Of course, I still grieve, but the darkness, hopelessness, and depression are gone. And whenever I feel those coming back, I return to what I know"—he raised his arms—"lifting my hands and voice in praise to the Lord."

> Nolan had learned that speaking praise is the way through the darkness into the light of breakthrough.
>
> Regardless of our dark circumstances, God is always worthy of praise.
>
> I will bless the Lord at all times; His praise shall continually be in my mouth. — Psalm 34:1

Nolan shared that just two months after his God-praising breakthrough, he was preparing breakfast for his five children when he heard a word from the Lord in his heart. "At first, I laughed and said, 'God, that can't be You!' The Lord had told me to take his children to McDonald's!" He chuckled and asked rhetorically, "Why would God tell anybody to go to McDonald's?! But I felt certain the message was from Him."

Nolan had learned that when you receive a *rhéma* (inner spoken word from God), you need to act on it. Often a *rhéma* word is time sensitive; it may fade if you don't respond quickly. So Nolan gathered his children and said, "We're going to McDonald's for breakfast!"

While ordering food amid the restaurant's chaos, a woman came in with five children. She and Nolan recognized each other immediately. They had attended the same college more than a decade earlier.

She offered her condolences for the loss of his wife, and Nolan thanked her. He asked about her husband, and she said he had passed away from cancer a few years earlier.

The two of them, single parents with a troop of ten children, sat down to reconnect and ate breakfast together.

Over the next few months, their friendship grew. A year later, they married, combining their large families.

Nolan said, "I still miss my wife, but God showed me that I can trust Him. I'm married again to a woman I love.

"I've learned that this world can be unpredictable. That life can throw all kinds of challenges at us. I've also learned that whatever comes, Jesus is my best friend, and I can trust Him."

Psalm 22:3 tells us God inhabits the praises of His people. Praise is not strictly a feeling or action; praise has *substance* and builds substance in the heavenly realm. Praise holds the power to break the bonds the enemy uses to entangle us. Where God is present, satan and his demons must depart. Thereby, the tormenting bonds are broken.

God is present in our praise.

Job experienced unprecedented loss, everything falling apart in his life after satan was allowed to attack him to the point of near death. The Bible says Job rose, tore his robe, shaved his head, and fell to the ground in *worship*. He said, "The Lord gave, and the Lord has taken away; *blessed be the name of the Lord*" (Job 1:21, author emphasis).

Even in Job's darkest moment—having lost his ten children in a tragic event, all his earthly possessions and wealth, and then his health—he *chose* to rise and praise God in faith.

We saw that principle in Nolan Reed's story. He'd lost his wife, but in truth, she was never truly his. She belonged to God.

Through praising, Nolan realized that the time they'd had together was a gift, and even though she had been his wife and was now in Heaven, she had always belonged to God.

The power of praise brought Nolan's breakthrough—just as Job experienced breakthrough when he surrendered his heart and all to the Lord in praise.

- Isaiah 61:3 teaches us that the "garment of praise" is the antidote for the "spirit of heaviness."
- In Psalm 30:5, we have this promise: "Weeping may endure for a night, but joy comes in the morning."
- Nehemiah 8:10 reminds us, "Do not sorrow, for the joy of the Lord is your strength."

When we praise God, the result is *joy*.

Unlike happiness, joy is not temporary or dependent on circumstances. Joy comes from God and can sustain us *through* the struggles of life when we choose to plant the seed of faith by praising Him.

As Job and Nolan praised God *through* their pain, thousands of years apart, their hearts, minds, and lives took a drastically new direction of blessing, proving that God and His Word are the same yesterday, today, and forever.

When we praise God, the result is breakthrough and joy.

If we hold on to grief or discouragement, allowing it to linger too long, giving it too much room to grow, and feeding it with our emotions, a spirit of depression, self-pity, and hopelessness comes to settle over us. For what we sow, we reap. God has given His people a superior spiritual weapon we can choose to use that keeps inner darkness away and joy sustained: praise.

When we're struggling, not feeling like praising God, a determination to praise Him anyway is often the faith step into breakthrough. We *choose* to take action in agreement with God, not by feeling but by faith. When we praise Him in *faith*, His Spirit rises within us, bringing His joy, peace, and presence, forcing out the spirit of heaviness.

Whatever you need, ask the Lord. Then praise Him in faith until your prayer is answered.

The next time you feel disheartened, disappointed, depressed, heartbroken, dejected, gloomy, miserable, desperate, or anything similar, remember that God has made a way for you:

Praise is your superior spiritual weapon.

Chapter 9

BREAKING BARRIERS TO ANSWERED PRAYER
NEAR DEATH IN THE KERN RIVER

> Your iniquities have separated you from
> your God; and your sins have hidden His
> face from you, so that He will not hear.
> — Isaiah 59:2

G OD PROMISES TO HEAR *AND ANSWER* OUR PRAYERS—
PROMISES THAT OFFER PROFOUND ENCOURAGEMENT
AND HOPE. However, these assurances come with a
frequently overlooked condition that can prevent our
prayers from reaching Heaven.

Feeling separated from God, having lost intimacy with
Him, usually means there is unconfessed sin blocking
our relationship with our righteous heavenly Father. We
feel the distance as though a wall is between us and God.

Unconfessed sin and lack of repentance *undermine* receiving answers to our prayers.

Once we've repented, we're in *right standing* with God through the blood and grace of Jesus and back in fellowship. Our faith is then connected to the power that can move mountains.

Repentance isn't about punishing ourselves by living under guilt and shame but rather *freeing us* to have a full relationship with God in a mindset and heartset of determined faith.

To repent means to turn away from choices that do not align with God's holy character and Word.

Though God is greatly loving and merciful, He is holy, requiring our righteousness. Repentance is not only genuine sorrow for having walked into disobedience, but is also changing our course to a path that agrees with God's Word and will.

That's why repentance should always be one of the actions we take before asking God for anything. Repentance restores and strengthens our relationship with our Father, enabling us to enjoy close fellowship with Him and have confidence that we are asking according to His will. When that occurs, He hears our prayers and will answer them.

The Bible emphasizes the importance of repentance, as in 1 John 1:9: "If we confess our sins, He is faithful and just to forgive us our sins and to cleanse us from all unrighteousness." God's forgiveness and grace are *gifts* He readily provides.

Be Grateful and Thankful

Attention to gratitude will remind us how much we already have and steer us from focusing on lack. A trap of satan we easily get caught in is wanting more, thinking that more success, money, or possessions will make us happy. But gratitude and giving thanks bring a godly perspective: seeing life as *filled with God's blessings.*

The Bible speaks against complaining and tells us to "Give thanks in all circumstances; for this is the will of God in Christ Jesus for you" (1 Thessalonians 5:18).

Being grateful and thanking God deepens our faith and keeps us grounded and focused on the truth. Even in difficult times, "the Lord is good" (Psalm 34:8).

Remembering His past faithfulness also strengthens our hope for the future, which is cause for being continually grateful and thanking Him.

The following story exposes the sobering reality that, despite receiving so much from God—including new physical and spiritual life—I reverted to selfish thinking, which placed *me* back on the throne over my life. I had unknowingly slipped back into a state of rebellion against God—a perilous position to occupy.

Whenever we claim the throne over our lives, making decisions without seeking God's will and guidance, He steps aside and waits for us to repent and invite Him to reign again as our Lord, King of kings.

Near Death in the Kern River

Nine months after surviving the airplane crash (detailed in my book *Flight To Heaven*), I experienced a near-drowning in the Kern River in California. That horrifying experience also left a lasting impression on me.

I was twenty.

Looking back, I believe I was struggling with ADHD, made worse by the months sequestered in a wheelchair and rehabilitation. Prior to the crash, I was an active athlete in various sports. So I was bursting with energy and razor-sharp focus, which was difficult for me to control, especially in that physically restrained circumstance.

At the time of the near drowning, my arm, though finally freed from the cast, was strapped to my waist and immobile. My leg was still in a cast, and my right eye vision was limited to blurry images. Yet my energy and the need for an outlet had reached an explosive level.

I was ravenous to resume physical activities when I came across a brochure about white water rafting on the Kern River. Excited, and despite my handicaps, I convinced a friend to buy a raft. Another friend volunteered to drive.

Our group of nineteen- and twenty-year-olds was ready for an adventure!

I called the California Department of Recreation and was told that rafting the Kern River in April would be like "signing a death warrant." I also learned that the river south of the lake was especially dangerous. Melting snow had increased the freezing water's depth to upwards of thirty feet and was fast-moving. The section north of the lake was reported to be only about two feet deep.

Our group of four had been close friends for over a year at college, and I wanted to show that I could still lead them on an adventure despite my injuries. I thought it would be a blast and a way to prove to myself that I was still the same fearless leader I'd always been.

In addition, I had been reading God's promises for gaining health and healing. Jesus said in Mark 11:23–24,

> "Whoever says to this mountain, 'Be removed and be cast into the sea,' and does not doubt in his heart, but believes that those things he says will be done, he will have whatever he says. Therefore I say to you, whatever things you ask when you pray, believe that you receive them, and you will have them."

Reading the passage for the first time had changed my thinking and life. The verses revealed something incredible: *God's Word is the foundation that holds the entire universe together!*

I was believing for complete healing, and even though I had quite a way to go, I was ready for an exhilarating adventure like the Kern River brochure offered.

My three close friends and I drove toward Kernville and stopped to survey a section of the Kern River. It was immediately apparent how treacherous the water was for rafting. We unanimously agreed that attempting it would be nothing short of suicide.

We got back in the car and about two miles downstream, we passed a section just south of the lake, close to the exact area I'd been warned was dangerous. However, as we looked at the stretch, I thought it looked safe enough. Without hesitation, I said, "Let's give it a try."

Mike and Larry immediately replied, "No way! You don't know what's down river!" But JT and I felt confident and a bit reckless. We decided to be the daring ones. Caught up in youthful excitement, we thought we could handle this slow-moving section. No problem.

In my eagerness to relieve some adrenaline, I overlooked caution. We didn't even have life jackets or much experience with river rafting.

JT had strength and determination, but I still had a full cast on my left leg, from foot to groin, as well as my other injuries. Nonetheless, I was sure I could somehow manage rafting. What a joke!

I climbed into the front of the raft, and JT took the back. I was the lookout, paddling with one arm, and JT used an oar as the rudder.

We moved slowly down the river, and I felt alive and free.

I thought it was odd that people on shore were yelling at us, "You don't want to do that!" and "You're seriously going through the rapids?!" We shrugged, confused by the ruckus. We were just having a thrill ride.

Someone pulled out a movie camera, a pretty rare sight in the early 1970s. I could see on JT's face that we both had the same thought. *We're impressing people! Wow! All the more reason to go for it!*

We felt like stars, seamlessly gliding at about two mph, some onlookers cheering, "Go for it!" and "You can do it!" Of course, the naysayers were still shouting protests. "Don't do it! You're crazy!" We laughed and gave thumbs-up.

I was becoming aware of my rapidly weakening body, turning my thoughts. *Oh man, I used to be so strong. . . . Now look at me!*

My muscles were gone, and I was skin and bones. But I wasn't going to let those thoughts stop me from enjoying our five or six minutes of fame.

Being filmed also added the pressure of not backing out. *No way!* Pride wouldn't let us. We felt like real action heroes!

Ten minutes in, the water was moving us faster, though the surface seemed calm. The thought that we could be in danger didn't cross our young and proud minds. The cameraman was now running alongside the river, filming us, and we felt cool.

Nothing we heard from the onlookers caused us any concern until some campers started yelling and pointing downriver. "Get out! There's a . . . ahead!" Their warnings didn't make sense, so we ignored them, paddling forward with a false sense of security. We didn't know that the water depth was thirty feet. We hadn't even thought about it or what might be ahead. We were coasting in the limelight as our speed increased.

As we rounded a bend, we heard a faint gravelly noise. It grew louder as the river picked up more speed and capped white. We didn't realize we were in trouble until the churning water became a massive roar. "We gotta get outta here!" JT shouted.

Frantically, we paddled toward the riverbank as the water fought us, sucking us back toward the center at about ten mph, overtaking our attempts to steer to safety, and more quickly picking up speed.

I paddled as strongly as possible with one arm and JT with all his strength. But we were no match for the river.

The cameraman and crowd now forgotten, my only thought was how little control we had over the boat, and my rising panic. Our speed was increasing, controlled by the accelerating current pulling us straight toward the awful roaring.

After a final, desperate attempt to gain control of the raft, we had no choice but to accept the inevitable. The roar consumed us, and we braced ourselves.

JT's wide eyes locked with mine for a split second, and in that moment, the roar seemed to go silent. We were hurled into a moment of nothingness that slammed us backward into free fall over a monstrous twenty-foot waterfall raging into a ninety-degree drop.

My only thought was survival.

My descent didn't stop until I was about thirty feet beneath the surface, pressed face-down against a massive rock, the falls' force pounding against my back, overpowering me and holding me hostage. I was trapped against a twelve-foot-wide boulder, black, cold, and mossy.

Lord! . . . I prayed, but not for help or a second chance. My thoughts centered on the fact that God had already saved me from a fatal airplane crash—a miracle survival I had flippantly lost sight of in my desire to be my old self again, seeking life's next rush of adventure. I felt unworthy to ask Him to save me again.

This one is my fault.

I immediately saw my pride and selfishness and felt the weight of shame, the power of the falls momentarily forgotten. There, trapped at the bottom of the Kern River, I recalled Jesus asking me something immediately after the airplane crash. "What will you do with the life I've given you?"

Now, face down at the end of my second chance at life, I thought my life was over. *This is it, my end. I've failed God. I've ignored every warning. I've again taken from Him control over my life.*

A recent memory flashed to mind—a phone call with my father just a few days prior.

We seldom spoke on the phone and had never been particularly close. He was a good man, but to me, not exactly warmhearted. In our last conversation, he'd cautioned me, "Dale, do you think you should go white water rafting? You haven't recovered much. You can't use your arm or leg. And besides, how do you know it's safe at this time of year?" I convinced him we'd stay in the recommended safe section of the river. I discounted his cautions.

Pinned to that rock at the bottom of the river, I replayed our conversation.

What's he going to think of me now?

There were no flashbacks of my life, no other memories. I was simply acutely aware of being trapped thirty feet under icy water only a degree or two above freezing.

Unable to breathe, unable to move, completely powerless, I was at the mercy of the waterfall's unstoppable force. More importantly, I was at the mercy of God, again at the edge of life.

Drowning in shame, I prayed, *God, I am so sorry. You owe me nothing. Please, . . . just forgive me. I can't believe*

I did this! You gave me every warning. I'm so sorry. You had plans for me, and I blew it. I caused this, and I'm not worthy to ask for Your help.

Time had stopped; my world had collapsed into God's hands, held at death's door by the falls' force against me. I had accepted that I was going to die within seconds.

I relaxed, released the air from my lungs, and let the icy water in. I felt no pain. Instead, I felt an incredible peace.

The experience defied all logic. I wasn't dead. I was still thinking and seeing when suddenly, I felt someone grab the back of my shirt. In less than a second, I was pulled to the water's surface.

> He sent from above, He took me;
> He drew me out of many waters.
> — Psalm 18:16

The moment I reached the surface, I thought I may live. I coughed out water and took in a deep gulp of air. But just as quickly, the undertow pulled me back down to the bottom of the river, where it dragged me downstream, face down, moving backward. My feet hit rocks again and again. I'd later learn that every toe on my casted foot was broken, and the big toe of my right foot.

I felt as if God was testing me, as if He was saying, "I brought you up supernaturally; now let's see what you'll do."

With just one arm functional, I fought with everything I had to reach the surface and breathe again.

At last, I broke through, gasping for air, and kept fighting, struggling to swim toward shore. That's when I saw Larry. He'd found a rope and threw it to me. I grabbed hold, and somehow, he pulled me to the riverbank.

Larry was talking nonstop. "Oh my gosh! I can't believe it! JT made it up fast, but you were underwater for at least three minutes!" Larry kept rattling on, but I was too dazed to focus. I sat there stunned and began to cry. I couldn't speak or otherwise react. I had come so close to death again and so soon after the airplane crash.

On the seven-hour drive back to campus, I barely said a word. I was lost in deep thought, trying to process what had happened.

After I returned to my dorm room, I told no one what had happened. The four of us knew what JT and I had been through, how close we'd come to death, but we hardly spoke about it again. It was as though we were stunned into silence.

All that mattered to me was that God had spared me—again. I was unspeakably grateful, but I struggled with my decisions on that near-fatal day.

The inside of my cast was soaked, but I was too ashamed to tell anyone what had happened, including my doctor.

I never told my dad, either. His warnings from the day before we rafted echoed relentlessly in my head.

About a month later, the cast was replaced due to the moisture and a consequential skin infection. The broken toes took months to heal. I was struggling with the physical setbacks of the second near-death experience, how God had saved me and why, and still greatly struggling with memory issues from the airplane crash. I felt my only option was to leave college and move back home.

As far as reconciling my second close call with death, I believed an angel had rescued me. Lying trapped on that boulder, I felt so ashamed of my pride and irresponsible actions that I didn't believe I should ask God to rescue me. Yet He did. He had a purpose for my life that I could not have begun to imagine.

That second near-death was a classic case of disobedience—my spirit saying no to God, my flesh saying yes to my immediate desires, and my ego convincing me *I'm still strong; I'm not that weak; I can still make an impression.*

In that Kern River "adventure" at age twenty, so young, God patiently continued to teach me the importance of obedience to Him, letting Him lead as I learned how to follow. Now in my seventies, I reflect on fifty years of refining my human errors through God's grace and guidance. Refining is an ongoing adventure of process.

Since that day at the bottom of Kern River, I've lived with this mindset: It's God's way or *no* way!

Surrender

Jesus taught that true faith involves surrendering our desires to God's will and following Him wholeheartedly.

When Jesus said, "If anyone would come after Me, let him deny himself, and take up his cross daily, and follow Me" (Luke 9:23), He was calling us, His followers, to a life of

- complete surrender,
- full commitment,

- total sacrifice,
- ongoing trust, and
- atomic faith.

We all have dreams, goals, and plans—gifts of choice given to us by God, who even spoke about those: "A man's heart plans his way, but the Lord directs his steps" (Proverbs 16:9).

Yet many accounts in the New Testament show that following Jesus sometimes means setting aside our plans to allow God to lead us into and through His greater plans. Jesus demonstrated this perfectly in the Garden of Gethsemane when He prayed, "Not My will, but Yours, be done" (Luke 22:42). He showed that surrender isn't about losing but *choosing* something greater: God's purpose.

When Jesus said in Luke 9:23, "Let him deny himself, and take up his cross daily," he meant accepting the challenges and sacrifices that come with choosing to follow Him instead of going our own way.

In Jesus's time, the cross symbolized suffering and obedience to God's will. That call is for us today, for everyone who fully surrenders to God and follows Jesus, not just in big moments but in everyday decisions.

When we face tough times, including frustrations such as putting aside our desires to help others, we take up our crosses. Such times should remind us of this truth:

Following Jesus isn't only about what we gain but what we're willing to give up.

Jesus didn't promise that following Him would be easy; He promised it would be *worth it*.

When we surrender to God, we gain a deeper relationship with Him. We find peace and purpose that reaches far beyond ourselves.

Surrendering to Jesus and picking up our crosses may sound challenging, but it's also freeing like no other freedom. We're no longer relying only on our strength and knowledge but on God's *supernatural* strength and wisdom in us.

Have you ever imagined having a superpower? That's what followers of Jesus Christ have—the greatest superpower, the power that moves life's mountains, heals the sick, and sets the captives of any burden free, no matter the challenge or its human statistics, whether physical, spiritual, mental, emotional, relational, or otherwise.

Shame and Guilt

Feeling shame and guilt can make us want to avoid God. When we know we've done wrong or feel that we've failed, we may think, *I don't deserve to go to God*, or *He won't listen to me*. Such feelings, while real, are not reasons to stay away from God. In fact, such thoughts and feelings should be reminders of exactly why we need Him and why He's faithfully always with us.

Regardless of what we've done and how ashamed we feel, God wants us to come to Him. He is our good Father.

He doesn't want us to run away and hide as Adam and Eve did. He invites us to bring our mistakes and willful sins to Him and ask Him for His forgiveness, healing, and help as we continue forward—with Him.

Imagine praying with unshakable confidence, knowing that every word reaches Heaven and returns with unstoppable power. How? It begins with a heart of repentance, surrender, and gratitude to God. By consistently seeking His forgiveness and clearing away unconfessed sin, you position yourself to receive swift, unmistakable answers to prayer—each and every time.

Chapter 10

STROKES OF FAITH
THE PAULA BLACK STORY

"By your words you will be justified, and
by your words you will be condemned."
— Matthew 12:37

Does What We Speak Matter? After All, They're Just Words

YES! What we speak matters greatly. The Bible has a lot to say about our words, and Jesus often taught His disciples about the power of the tongue.

Our spoken words are one of the key ways we express our faith in action—our agreement with God.

"Assuredly, I say to you, whoever *says* to this mountain, 'Be removed and be cast into the sea,' and does not doubt in his heart, but believes that those things he *says* will be done, he will have whatever he *says*." — Mark 11:23 (author emphasis)

Words Create

When God created the heavens and the Earth, He *spoke* them into existence. Speaking is an action. Throughout God's acts of creation, He spoke, "Let there be," and there was! Our all-powerful God chose *speaking* as His faith action to create the worlds, humanity, light, and all that exist.

What can be more shocking and powerful than this Scripture? "Death and life are in the power of the tongue" (Proverbs 18:21).

Jesus spoke words of life that healed, delivered, and established truth. Since we are created in God's image (Genesis 1:26) and instructed to imitate Jesus (Ephesians 5:1), shouldn't we also speak words of life? Since God created the world with nothing but spoken words, shouldn't we use spoken words based on what we believe in harmony with God's Word? Words are a major key to how our prayers get answered.

God did not simply *think* what He wanted to create. He took action by *speaking* creation into existence. If we are to imitate our Creator, we should speak words of faith out loud, not simply *think* them.

Where do our words come from? They originate in our hearts. Then we choose to speak aloud what we *believe*. "For out of the abundance of the heart the mouth speaks" (Matthew 12:34).

Heart Talk

What do we believe in our hearts?

What words are we thereby speaking to ourselves?

Are we speaking the truth according to God or repeating the enemy's lies?

How we speak to ourselves matters because words create. Yes, all words. How we speak to ourselves is what I call *heart talk*.

God gave us the power to choose what we will reflect in our self-talk and actions: death or life, blessings or curses, darkness or light (Deuteronomy 30:19). We also have the power to change things by our faith in action, using spoken words. With such creative authority available to us, God reminds us of our responsibility to manage our tongues to stay in *agreement* with His Word and will.

> "I say to you, whatever things you ask when you pray, believe that you receive them, and you will have them." — Mark 11:24

Remember, satan continually tries to direct our words in ways that will *rob us* of victories like answered prayer. He manipulates humankind to agree with his will—destruction. He tempts us to use our words for outcomes of defeat, lack, sickness, loneliness, pain, fear, and doubt.

Jesus compared satan's work of death to His work of life:

> "The thief does not come except to steal, and to kill, and to destroy. I have come that they may have life, and that they may have it more abundantly." — John 10:10

Every person faces two choices in life, leading to opposite outcomes. One path leads to destruction and death, and the other leads to victory and the abundant life God designed for us.

You have the power to choose for yourself, each moment, what you will believe in your heart and express through spoken words.

Words Are Seeds

In Mark 4, Jesus taught His disciples that words are seeds that produce fruit. What seed words are you planting in your life?

Though Jesus told us we will face persecution, tribulation, and temptation, *we have a choice in our outcomes!*

The Bible says, "Death and life are in the power of the tongue, and those who love it will eat its fruit" (Proverbs 18:21). In this proverb, we learn that the outcomes we experience depend on the type of thoughts and words we plant.

The Paula Black Story

Paula was in the prime of her life—a wife, mother, and businesswoman—when she heard the dreaded words: "It's cancer." The doctors said it was aggressive and terminal.

Doctors gave her three to six months to live.

At that time, I was serving as senior pastor of a growing church a couple of years after my aviation career. I took leave from everything to be Paula's full-time cancer researcher and a more available husband to help care for her and encourage her in the battle she faced.

Paula and I began learning everything we could about her fatal disease. We spent hours at the library daily, tirelessly researching all conventional and alternative cancer treatments available. We met with doctors and oncologists and spoke with cancer patients and their families.

Mostly, we prayed.

During that research season, God led Paula and me into what became known as the BODY-SOUL-SPIRIT Approach to healing and wellness. This method deals with the whole person and treats the root causes of the disease, not just the symptoms.

> God created every person in His image and as a three-part being that we are to care for:
>
> • You are a spirit.
>
> • You have a soul (mind, will, emotions).
>
> • You live in a temporary physical body.
>
> If you choose Jesus as your Savior, His Spirit takes up residence in your heart, giving you access to all He provides for your body, soul, and spirit.

Twenty months after Paula's initial diagnosis, her advanced-stage cancer was gone! Completely gone! Without chemotherapy, without radiation, without drugs, and without additional surgery. Her entire story is available in an easy-to-read book, *Life, Cancer and God.*

Paula got her life back.

Her healing defied medical statistics. Her atomic faith, heart talk, and bringing her body back into agreement with God's design reversed her terminal cancer—permanently. At this writing, that was twenty-seven years ago. Learn more about Paula's journey at PaulaBlack.org.

Eleven Years Later

A series of events triggered a host of stresses in Paula's life. A couple of family deaths—her father's and mine within five weeks—and then a monumental move, relocating to a different state.

Amid the whirlwind, Paula was involved in a major transaction as a real estate agent—one she was counting on for our family's financial stability. When she went to collect the money from escrow, she was blindsided by devastating news. The deal had fallen through without warning and at the last second. The funds she had expected to receive had vanished.

The financial strain heaped on everything else she was carrying proved too much.

We had just pulled up in front of our home when Paula, sitting in the car's passenger seat, suddenly felt a strange sensation in her head, like a flash flood rushing over her. She explained, "It feels like waves flowing through my brain." There was no pain, but definitely something wasn't right. "I feel tipsy, like my body's betraying me," she said, describing a dizzy, disoriented feeling. "My body feels completely foreign to me."

Her entire left side felt numb. Her limbs had no strength, and she couldn't move properly. The simple task of walking into the house and up the stairs to the bedroom seemed impossible. Leaning on the railing with her right arm while I supported her weight and balance, she painstakingly dragged her left leg up the stairs, step after step.

Her speech had begun to slur, another sign that something was seriously wrong. "I realized my body was reacting to the stress I was under." She knew how dangerous stress was.

Paula was facing another life-altering health event. Her knowledge of God's Word and His will for healing was already firmly established in her heart. Having previously won the battle against terminal cancer, her experience of atomic faith once again kicked in.

In the face of this terrifying situation, Paula did what had become automatic since her life-threatening cancer battle: She persistently prayed, brought her words into agreement with God's promises, and spoke aloud the will of God with atomic faith.

"Despite what's happening in my body, I believe in the power of prayer, so I won't let fear consume me." She continued speaking God's promises about wholeness and healing and insisted that her body come into agreement with God's will. Based on her previous experiences of standing firm in faith, her mindset was that the symptoms were temporary and healing was her spiritual inheritance.

The following morning, a similar sensation washed over Paula's brain, causing her symptoms to worsen.

I called our daughter, Kara, and she left her job to help us get to a local hospital. On the way, as if the situation couldn't get worse, Paula suffered a third stroke. The same eerie washing sensation but stronger. She now had little to no control over her left arm and leg.

Immediately upon arriving at the emergency room, the medical team conducted an MRI to assess the damage. Over the next six hours, Paula went through multiple tests, and doctors told us she should stay two or three days, possibly longer.

Amid it all, Paula looked at me and said, "Please, Dale, would you take charge? I can't think straight."

Even in that vulnerable moment and weakened physical state, Paula's faith and determination didn't waver. She knew her fight was just beginning, but she was strong in her belief in God and His promises for healing, as He had faithfully proven with the unprecedented victory over terminal cancer.

Ultimately, that same day, Kara and I took Paula home, contrary to doctors' wishes.

We had a Bible study scheduled for that evening at our home, which Paula insisted we not cancel. Determined to stay with the plan, she refused to be a victim. "I've asked God for healing according to His Word, and I believe I'm healed despite my current symptoms. So I need to do everything I would if I were well."

That evening, everyone noticed Paula's symptoms and asked questions. However, she only briefly mentioned her situation during the group's prayer time, requesting prayers of agreement for her complete recovery.

Though her physical struggle was apparent by her shuffling, spilling, and dropping things, her faith remained unwavering. Her determined goal was to live her belief physically to the best of her ability. And she did. She continued putting her faith into action, refusing to be defined by or give power to her circumstances or symptoms.

Though she took leave from her real estate business, Paula insisted on continuing ministry work in our home office despite having suffered three ministrokes. She was physically struggling but continued her responsibilities.

For three months, our office felt like a crisis zone. "Things were chaotic as I naturally made countless mistakes, including sending books to the wrong people and emails full of typos." She now laughs. "Everything I did took much longer to accomplish than normal."

Determined, Paula repeatedly stated, "I'm healed in Jesus's name, and in faith, I need to do everything I would if I were completely well—to the best of my ability."

Within a few weeks, her condition began to improve slightly. Three months later, she had regained more strength and control over her left side. She continued thanking God, employing heart talk by claiming, "I am healed according to the teachings of Jesus!"

As much as possible, Paula lived as though she was already healed, but the journey wasn't easy. "My left foot and leg often felt like they were on fire as the nerves came back to life." The pain was excruciating each day.

Several months passed before she felt and moved relatively normally again. Even though her hope and belief were that healing is always God's will, the battle was difficult.

"The most challenging aspect was keeping my *belief* strongly alive, agreeing with God's Word that healing was mine. Several times, each and every day, I read Scripture promises and often stated, 'I am completely healed'—even though the stroke symptoms were still present."

Without Paula's solid belief in the integrity of God's living Word, her faith actions would have been empty. "I had to choose daily, sometimes hourly, what I believed: the Word of God or the symptoms." She read Bible promises about healing—often and *aloud*—because she understood that faith comes by hearing the Word of God (Romans 10:17).

Her faith was only as effective as her belief. She was choosing to act in faith according to what she believed, contrary to her physical symptoms.

Throughout the physical struggle, she relied on a collection of Scriptures that reinforced her hope and belief in healing. In faith, she read the healing promises out loud several times daily. (A download of Healing Scripture Promises can be accessed at DaleBlack.org.)

As with any battle, fear and temptation were constant companions, especially since many people told her, "Strokes only get worse." Family, friends, and medical personnel all shared similar thoughts: "People who suffer strokes often experience more strokes and eventually die from them."

Paula rejected all statements that were contrary to God's will in His Word. She responded by quoting Scripture such as 1 Peter 2:24, "By whose stripes you were healed," and others, including Mark 5:34, "Daughter, your faith has made you well. Go in peace, and be healed of your affliction."

When hit by anything that robs Paula of health, she chooses God's way—the abundant life Jesus offers. She says, "I knew the choice was always mine to make. One of my favorite Scriptures is Deuteronomy 30:19: 'I have set before you life and death, blessing and cursing; therefore choose life, that both you and your descendants may live.'"

In the end, she triumphed over the strokes, just as she had overcome terminal cancer! Slowly but steadily, her health was completely restored.

Paula's victory over both highlights the critical importance of *hope, belief,* and *faith*—atomic faith.

Now, ten years later, she remains completely free of symptoms and the residual effects common from strokes. She's fully recovered and leading a normal and healthy life—proof of the power of God's Word with unwavering *atomic faith.*

Every person individually chooses the words they'll believe and speak and the actions they'll take. So I must ask this vital question: Are you physically sick and struggling with a medical condition that doctors have said is getting worse?

Heart talk is faith in action that establishes what is believed through the creative power of words.

Instead of seeing yourself as "sick" and *trying* to get well, think of your situation from Heaven's perspective: Through the stripes of Jesus, your healing is assured—if you cultivate and nourish the seeds of faith within your heart.

The journey may be long, so remember these truths at every turn:

- Satan is trying to oppress you with sickness and disease, which are of his kingdom, this world.
- Jesus said the thief [satan, our enemy] comes to steal, kill, and destroy.
- Jesus came to bring you the abundant life of His kingdom, Heaven, for your spirit, soul, and body.
- You have a choice which kingdom you'll agree with.

Remember Romans 12:2:

> Do not be conformed to this world, but *be* transformed by the *renewing of your mind*, that you may *prove* what is that good and acceptable and perfect will of God. (author emphasis)

God's will is healing. But He did not say *He* would transform us; He gave us the power and authority to transform ourselves through our faith in His Word.

Abundant life is forged through acts of faith—by renewing your mind and aligning your actions with God's promises.

Take note: I am not describing a "name it and claim it" doctrine. I'm describing the teachings of Jesus for answered prayer that have always been in His Word but hidden by satan through false teaching and distractions from the Word. God's powerful principles were given to us, His children, so we could live the abundant life He provides.

A reliable study indicated that the average person has about forty thousand to fifty thousand thoughts daily, and about 70 percent are negative. However, the study also revealed that exceptional professional athletes reduced their self-talk to twenty thousand thoughts or less daily, with 50 percent of those thoughts positive.

Focused thinking and self-talk that agree with God's Word are critical to moving your thoughts from a victim mindset to an overcomer mindset, from a worldly mindset to an abundant life mindset.

By renewing your mind, you can change from victim living to victory living.

Your belief system is created by what you *say* inwardly and outwardly—your heart talk. Heart talk is based on the principle of Proverbs 23:7, "For as he thinks in his heart, so is he."

We receive what we believe!

- Paula did not allow herself to speak as a stroke or cancer victim.
- She did not allow others to treat her as a patient, invalid, or even sick.

- She rejected the identity of "having cancer" and "being a stroke victim."
- Instead, she chose to look at the diagnoses as curses, contrary to God's Word and His blessings.
- Paula stood firm on the belief that she was healed by faith in the completed work of Jesus.

Jesus directs us to *choose* how we see ourselves: sick or healed. Imperative is staying aware of our thoughts to ensure we make choices and take actions that agree with what God has said about us.

> Casting down arguments and every high thing that exalts itself against the knowledge of God, bringing every thought into captivity to the obedience of Christ. — 2 Corinthians 10:5

God has placed limitations on satan:
- He can attack, but through Jesus, we have superior power to overcome.
- He can rob, but through Jesus, we have superior power to be restored.

God's healing power and will to heal are constant and unchangeable, like gravity. Heaven and Earth may pass away, but God's Word endures forever.

Your faith bridges the gap between your prayers and their answers.

Chapter 11

FAITH'S POWER OVER ADDICTION
THE JOHNNY CASH STORY

For as he thinks in his heart, so is he.
— Proverbs 23:7

BELIEF IS THE DEEP CONVICTION OR TRUST IN SOMETHING, OFTEN WITHOUT NEEDING TANGIBLE PROOF AS EVIDENCE. In everyday life, belief is a powerful motivator that influences thoughts, decisions, and actions and shapes perceptions of what's possible. Belief can drive us to pursue goals that others may consider unattainable. Belief strengthens our resolve by fostering a sense of purpose and confidence, helping us overcome obstacles and achieve personal growth.

In the context of biblical faith, belief is the foundation of a spiritual journey, offering hope and guiding principles in the face of uncertainty.

What you believe is what you repeatedly say to yourself.

Let's pause for a moment and consider the day-to-day reality of that truth. Our thoughts affect our decisions, which steer our actions and shape who we are as individuals.

For example, after my plane crash, what if I had repeatedly told myself, *Dale, you're never going to walk again. You'll never again have your previous brain capability to store new information. And all the aviation training you stored prior—it's all gone. Erased! You might as well say goodbye to your dreams of piloting commercial jet airliners.*

Even though doctors had told me exactly that, if I had allowed myself to think in that negative, limited way, such thinking would have shaped me into a completely different person. I would be living an entirely different life, just as our key Scripture verse states. Personalized, the verse means this: As Dale thinks in his heart, so is he.

Such thinking would have caused me to miss out on almost every extraordinary, supernatural adventure I've had with God! I would have bypassed countless blessings. And there would be no books sharing those inspiring true stories that point to the power of aligning our thinking and will with our Lord's thinking and will.

God created humankind with the freedom and ability to choose who we are by how we think. He explained how this works and how powerful our thoughts are.

Our thinking is also strongly influenced by the active world around us. If TV commercials and other repetitive advertising weren't effective in selling products, no one would pay to air and print them.

Ask yourself: *What am I continually advertising and selling to my subconscious, my inner person?*

The subconscious mind is incapable of judging. It simply records data and experiences as they happen and believes the information is true. Unfortunately, satan uses this against us. He's called an evil genius for good reason. He designed a negative marketing campaign to sell you on your failures and get you to agree and submit to his negative reports. (Read John 8:44.)

- Do not believe the father of lies.
- Do not repeat the lies he ceaselessly tries to plant in your mind.
- Do not let his lies take root in your heart.
- Pull out his seeds of accusation by immediately rejecting them.
- In their place, plant the seeds of truth—God's promises from the Bible.

It Is Written

God's Word is the only way to successfully reject and counter satan's temptations and accusations. When Jesus was in the wilderness, tempted repeatedly by satan, He began his rebuttal each time with these three words: "It is written."

Why not do the same?

Renew your mind and be transformed.

The way to accomplish renewing your mind is by learning what the Word of God says and believing it.

- *Learn* from God's Word what He says about you.
- *Learn* from His Word what He says is possible for you.
- *Repeatedly* choose to believe what God wrote.

Speak out loud the *logos* (written) promises of the Bible so you hear them. Remember, "Faith comes by hearing, and hearing by the word of God" (Romans 10:17).

Will satan cease tempting you to believe his lies? Of course not. Will the world cease advertising? No way. So what do you do? Renew your thinking with a mindset and heartset rooted in the truth—the *logos* Word of God. And when you're tempted to think negatively about yourself or your situation, start your heart talk with, "It is written."

What we choose to believe is most often what we'll then choose to act on, shaping who we become and how we live. Remember, as a person thinks in their heart, so are they.

What do you need in your life? What is the obstacle you're struggling with?

> Jesus looked at them and said to them, "With men this is impossible, but with God all things are possible." — Matthew 19:26.

All things *are* possible!

Answers to prayer don't simply show up. They're the result of what you hope for, what you believe in your heart, and what you act on with faith.

In the 1970s, I was deeply inspired by Johnny Cash, the famous country singer, and by his unwavering faith. His incredible triumph over drug addiction, especially by going "cold turkey," was nothing short of remarkable. Without rehab or gradual reduction, Johnny's complete turnaround came solely through faith in God and His Word.

Against all odds, Johnny continued to live a long, purposeful, and meaningful life. His story, which I first read in *Guideposts* magazine, remains a powerful testament to faith and transformation.

The Johnny Cash Story

(A paraphrase of "Guideposts Classics: Johnny Cash on Overcoming Addiction"[8]*)*

Johnny jolted awake, his eyes fixed on the ceiling. He was fighting sickness, struggling to piece together what had happened. Standing beside him was an old man who asked, "Are you feeling better now, Mr. Cash?"

Johnny tried to respond, but his mind was clouded. His body felt heavy, and the old man's voice seemed distant. Slowly, Johnny sat up, forcing himself to make sense of the situation. "Ready for what?" he asked, assuming he'd been arrested again, most likely because of the pills.

That wasn't his first time in a jail cell. Back in 1965, Johnny crossed into Mexico to score pills—drugs he needed just to feel alive. On the way back, an El Paso customs agent caught him. His first night in jail followed, but the judge showed mercy, giving him a one-year suspended sentence. That was a wake-up call, but not the one that would change Johnny's life.

The world soon learned that Johnny Cash was a drug addict. In truth, he'd been hooked for five years.

He'd started with pep pills to stay high enough for his shows. Then he used depressants to sleep. He was living in overdrive, sprinting through life without a second to pause.

Friends begged him to slow down, but Johnny thought he knew better. His career demanded too much, and he turned to drugs for relief—a decision that would consume him.

At first, the pills felt like magic. They gave him energy, sharpened his senses, and made him feel invincible. But over time, the highs weren't as high. The few pills he took every day increased to a habit of several pills, then dozens, as he chased a feeling that no longer existed. He had become anxious, irritable, and sick. His weight plummeted and sleep was elusive. Depressants offered fleeting moments of peace, but they were hollow. He was in a constant cycle of cravings, never satisfied.

Before every show, Johnny was a nervous wreck. He no longer trusted himself on stage. If someone said, "You did great, Johnny!" he doubted them. If he was told, "Poor performance, Johnny," he believed that. He was lost and unable to see the truth in anything.

His addiction was killing him and destroying his life, and he knew it. Friends had died from the same struggle, and he saw the writing on the wall. He would be next unless something changed.

He and his career weren't the only things suffering. He was letting down the people closest to him—his band, crew, family, and friends. He missed shows, lost trust, and started burning through goodwill. But even with all the love and support around him, Johnny felt nothing and he no longer cared. Not about his career. Not about his family. Not about himself.

That's the way addiction works. It doesn't only leave you chasing a craving; addiction consumes your life, your identity, and your future and puts you in debt to something. Addiction begins to own you.

> Owe no one anything except to love one another.
> — Romans 13:8

Johnny knew he was heading for an early grave, the only outcome for someone in his shoes. He hated his life but saw no way out.

His friends, desperate to save him, suggested he enter a mental health institution. That idea hit him hard. He was teetering on the edge but didn't want to fall. So he ran.

He jumped into his car, pills stashed in his pocket, and drove south from Tennessee. He crossed the state line into Georgia, lost in his drug haze. The next thing he knew, he was staring at the ceiling of a jail cell.

"How did I get here?" he asked the old jailer.

"One of the night men picked you up," the man replied. "Found you stumbling around the streets and brought you in so you wouldn't hurt yourself."

Johnny followed him down the hall and into an office. "How much time am I gonna get for this?" He expected the worst.

The jailer shook his head. "You're doing time right now, Mr. Cash. And it's the worst kind." He handed Johnny an envelope. "Here are your things."

As Johnny pocketed his belongings, the old man added, "I'm a fan, Johnny. Always admired you. It's a shame to see you like this. I've heard stories but didn't know it was this bad."

Johnny had heard the same from his friends, his manager, and even strangers. He'd just shrugged it off, but the jailer wasn't done. "I don't know where you think you got your talent, Johnny, but if you believe God gave it to you, you're wreckin' the body He put it in."

That hit Johnny harder than anything else. Something shifted in him.

He walked out of the jailhouse and stood in the warm sun, looking at the jail and then his life. He knew he was better than this. Somewhere deep down, hope had finally stirred.

Johnny believed the Bible was alive and that Jesus was the Messiah. He'd been raised to understand the gospel message and amazing benefits of following Jesus, but he had strayed.

Standing before the jailhouse, he remembered 1 Corinthians 6:19: "Know ye not that your body is the temple of the Holy Spirit?" The Scripture echoed in his mind. He had been treating his body like everything but a temple. The drugs had taken control of his free will, but he realized he could take that back with God's help.

He got in his car and sat there. For the first time in years, Johnny prayed. He asked God to help him break free from the chains of addiction. He knew that getting sober and staying sober wouldn't be easy, but he believed sobriety was God's will.

Johnny's renewed belief and prayer action planted a small seed of faith in him.

When he returned to Nashville, he told his wife, June, and his friend, Marshall Grant, "I'm done with the drugs. Cold turkey. I need your help. Pray with me; read the Bible to me. And if I can't sleep, just sit with me and *pray*."

And pray they did.

With the help of a strong believer, Johnny learned about hope, belief, and faith. He was on a crash course to build his faith for deliverance from addiction.

He went through withdrawal—the pain, the sleepless nights—but he didn't touch another pill. With the power of prayer, his family's love, and his hope, belief, and growing faith in God's power, Johnny Cash kicked his habit for good.

From that day forward, he shared his freedom story with others. Whenever he met someone struggling with addiction, he'd tell them, "Give God's temple back to Him. The alternative is death."

He became known for spreading the good news and overcoming strongholds through faith in Jesus.

With God and with faith in His promises, there is always hope.

At the beginning of Johnny's healing journey, he used heart talk by quoting Matthew 4:4 as a personal statement of faith: "It is written, 'Man shall not live by bread alone but by every word that proceeds from the mouth of God.'"

Johnny Cash lived the rest of his life free of drugs. He led a rich and meaningful life that reflected God's glory through his music and lifestyle. His victory over addiction further proves that nothing is impossible with God. We can activate God's power within us by faith in action.

God Has a Way of Escape

No matter how trapped we feel, God always provides a way of escape for anyone who trusts in Him and His Word (1 Corinthians 10:13).

Godly heart talk toward escape of any kind—disease, addiction, sin, etc.—has never been more important than now. Satan, ruling and persuading this world, tempts us every day in ways that cloud our minds and draw us further from God's presence. Satan's deception and our acceptance of his lies are always the beginning of destruction. We *will* be deceived if we are not pursuing God's Word as truth. As the adage goes:

If you don't believe in something, you'll fall for anything.

God created all of us to believe—and He gave us the choice to determine our beliefs. Hopefully, you've chosen to believe God's Word:

- Jesus is God's Son.
- He died on the cross in your place.

- If you accept His free gift of salvation, you will have the power of His Spirit within you and eternal life with Him.

Once you've believed and accepted Jesus as your Savior, God gives you access to every benefit and blessing He provides for His children.

> Bless the Lord, O my soul,
> And forget not all His benefits:
> Who forgives all your iniquities,
> Who heals all your diseases,
> Who redeems your life from destruction,
> Who crowns you with lovingkindness and tender mercies.
> — Psalm 103:2–4

The power of Jesus available for our access is greater than any other power in this world. His power can overcome satan and all things that trap us, rob us, and hurt us.

> Whatever is born of God overcomes the world; and this is the victory that has overcome the world—our faith. — 1 John 5:4

Do Not Be Deceived

Our entire world is growing ever darker, like the black, angry clouds I've often flown through as a jet pilot. They can obscure vision, cause confusion, and tempt us to fear.

The Bible describes a powerful, *deluding* influence that will capture all vulnerable people in the last days—even some of God's people will be deceived (Matthew 24:24).

Only by knowing what is true can we recognize what is false.

God's Word is true.

We've each been given the assignment of gatekeeper over our minds and hearts. No one else can do this job for us. Those who intend to challenge and take down any thoughts contrary to God's must be on guard every moment and take these three actions:

1. Determine what you'll allow yourself to see, hear, and think.
2. Learn what the Bible teaches so you know what is true.
3. Keep your thoughts and decisions in agreement with truth: God's character, His Word, and His will.

Until recent years, much of the evil in our world was hidden beneath the surface. No longer so; evil is evident and expanding rapidly. Evil is so rampant that *right looks wrong* and *wrong looks right*. The days of darkness and confusion prophesied long ago have arrived. But there's good news. We can understand and confidently know what is true and right if we learn the Word of God.

The message of hope, if you're a follower of Jesus, is this: You are God's child, which means that *Jesus lives in you*. You also have access to His supreme power, the promise of abundant life now on this earth and eternal life.

Through Jesus, you have within you the power and authority to disarm the devil! While satan constantly lies to you, remember that he has no authority or power over you—unless you give those to him by believing his lies.

In guarding the gateway of your heart and mind, obey God diligently: "Submit to God. Resist the devil and he will flee from you" (James 4:7).

Remember:

With God, nothing is impossible!

PART FOUR

Living By Faith

Chapter 12

EVERYDAY MIRACLES OF FAITH
THE STORIES OF THE LOST CAMERA AND EARRING

"If you ask anything in My name, I will do it."
— John 14:14

Jesus Hears Your Prayers

YEARS AGO, I SAT ALONE IN AN AIRPORT, WAITING FOR THE WEATHER TO CLEAR. Looking out the window, I noticed a casket being loaded into a jet airliner's pressurized cargo compartment. My thoughts wandered to Lazarus's tomb and Jesus standing in that scene. I tried to recall what He said after His friend's gravestone had been rolled away, but His words had escaped me.

Curious and eager to remember, I reached into my flight case and pulled out my red-letter New Testament. I knew that every Word of the Savior held significance whatever the situation. Jesus was standing before the tomb of Lazarus with many people watching, hoping, and wondering what He might do.

What had Jesus said before raising Lazarus from death? I knew I'd be moved by His words when I rediscovered the answer.

Jesus Uses Words—Faith in Action

Lazarus had been in the tomb for four days before Jesus arrived to demonstrate God's glory and His authority over life and death.

Jesus lifted His eyes toward Heaven and said, "Father, I thank You that You have heard Me" (John 11:41). The verse reminds us that prayer is not only about asking but also about recognizing God's faithfulness and thanking Him for His faithful listening and responding.

Jesus continued, "Because of the people who are standing by I said this, that they may believe that You sent Me" (v. 42).

Jesus made clear that His actions of faith—through His words—served a purpose beyond the immediate miracle He was orchestrating. He wanted the witnesses to believe in His divine mission—that He was sent by God as the Messiah.

Then Jesus spoke with a loud voice, "Lazarus, come forth" (v. 43)!

The authority of His *rhēma* word is a recurring theme in Scripture, reminding us of the power of God's spoken word to create, heal, and restore.

Lazarus emerged, and Jesus said, "Loose him, and let him go" (v. 44), indicating his grave clothes.

In the same way Lazarus was freed from the burial binding, believers are freed from our bonds of sin and death through Jesus Christ.

Exercise Your Authority in Jesus

An important aspect of faith is authority. Unless you understand your spiritual authority through your relationship with Jesus, your faith will be uncertain, weak, and ineffective.

Jesus said, "Whatever you ask in My name, that I will do" (John 14:13).

"In My name" (NKJV) is translated in the Amplified Bible "as My representative." The deeper meaning of the phrase is important to understand: the authority of His name *and* all that His name represents.

When you pray and take faith action based on who Jesus is and all that He represents, and when you ask in Jesus's name with the understanding of His authority, you and God become united in agreement. That uniting is necessary to ignite atomic faith that will accomplish what you and God have agreed on.

The Story of the Lost Camera

In the summer of 1981, a trip to La Paz, Mexico, would become an unforgettable experience for Paula, our two children, and me. The trip was twofold: a family vacation and a mission to assess whether our aviation company could support a local orphanage. We were looking forward to some fun sport fishing in the Sea of Cortez, and we intended to give supplies to local churches to distribute to those in need.

Our family and a few volunteers boarded a beautiful Learjet 35A, and I piloted us to Mexico from Long Beach, California.

We often flew teams of volunteers to various destinations to distribute gospel tracts, food, and clothing and to provide various types of assistance throughout South and Central America and Mexico.

But this trip became an unexpected lesson in faith.

Upon landing in La Paz, we loaded into a couple of taxis with outreach supplies and our luggage. Soon we checked into the Los Arcos Hotel, where I had stayed numerous times.

Once we'd arrived in our room and were unpacking our bags, I realized something was missing: an aluminum waterproof case that safely carried my highly prized 35mm camera and professional photo equipment.

That wasn't just any camera; it had documented many incredible moments—beginning in the jungles of northern Peru and throughout many amazing adventures worldwide. I had carried that beloved camera for over twelve years, capturing spectacular images and memories of family, aviation, and missions. The loss would be devastating.

Paula and I retraced our steps, but the search was unsuccessful. We concluded we must have overlooked the case when unloading the taxi.

There were always about fifty taxis lined up at the airport, so we had no idea which one we'd taken or how to find it. We started checking with every cab driver in sight. Driver after driver shook their heads and gave the same answer: "It's gone. This is Mexico. You'll never see that camera again."

The easy decision at that pivotal juncture would have been to give up the search, agree with statistics, and bear the loss in my heart. But that way of thinking wasn't part of the lifestyle we had adopted; it wasn't how we'd come to operate with God. We'd been practicing unyielding faith, and this situation offered another opportunity.

Once the stark realization of the missing camera hit us, Paula and I joined hands and prayed. We took authority over the camera in Jesus's name. The camera was our property, and we knew we had a spiritual right to expect it to be returned. So we asked God to bring the camera back, and we believed He was answering our prayer.

At that moment of initial prayer, our quest for the camera transformed into an act of faith, anchored in belief rather than mere hope.

We thought about offering a reward, but I quickly dismissed the idea. The lost camera became a test of atomic faith, like all challenges that seem impossible to overcome. We neither offered nor hinted at any reward.

Each time we asked a taxi driver if he knew of a camera left in a taxi, we were told, "It's gone," and "Forget about it." Every person seemed convinced that the camera was lost for good.

We spent the next three days in La Paz, balancing fishing with discussions about the orphanage. We also met with a few pastors of local churches and handed off supplies for them to distribute.

Each day, I'd ask the front desk attendant, "Has anyone found a camera?" They always shook their head and replied, "No, amigo. Nada."

Throughout our busy days, we informed every cab driver we met about the missing camera. We had asked God to bring our camera back to us, and we knew He'd heard our prayers. We were careful not to speak any words contrary to our prayers of faith.

On the morning of our departure, I again checked with the hotel manager a final time. Again, the man shook his head, "No, señor. Lo siento."

Still holding strongly to the reins of atomic faith, we packed our bags and headed to the airport to return home. Settled in the cab, I asked our driver, "Have you heard anything about a camera left in a taxi several days ago?" The driver shook his head, and again we received the familiar response. "You'll never see that camera again, señor. These things get sold quickly."

The driver stopped at the Learjet, and we began loading our cargo. I asked Paula to handle the boarding process while I did the preflight checks. When everything was secured and everyone seated, I was about to start the engines when I saw a man running on the tarmac toward us. "Señor! Señor!" he yelled, waving an arm.

At first, I didn't recognize him. Then it hit me. He was the taxi driver who had picked us up when we'd first arrived. He'd had the camera all along.

I could tell by his body language that he was eager to hand it over. Tucked tightly into the bend of his arm was the unmistakable aluminum case.

My camera! Turning to Paula with a grin, I said, "Could you go get the case?"

"You mean the camera?" she replied with a smile. She stepped outside, thanked the man, and took the case. As he turned to leave, Paula asked, "Do you mind waiting a moment?" He nodded, and she carried the case onto the plane.

We opened it and to our amazement, every single piece of equipment was perfectly intact—the camera, lenses, filters. . . . Nothing was missing.

I stood there humbled and in awe. The man had returned my camera without hope of getting something in return because no reward had been offered during our searching. Yet the case had almost seemed hot in his hands, as if he couldn't wait to be rid of it. His actions clearly reflected the work of the Spirit of God.

When God answers prayers of faith and fulfills His promises, nothing—not time, circumstance, or even human will—can stand in the way.

There was one more thing I needed to do.

I had promised God that when the camera was returned, I'd bless the person who brought it back. I secured the plane and handed control over to the copilot for the time being, and our family stepped out and walked to the patiently waiting man.

We warmly thanked the man for returning the camera.

I asked his name and for permission to pray for him. With my hands on his shoulders, I thanked God for answering our prayers and for Ricardo's honesty and integrity. I prayed for his family, business, and future and asked the Lord to pour blessings over every part of his life. Tears filled his eyes as we embraced him.

I had earlier prepared a gift for whoever returned the camera and kept that plan to myself. As a final gesture, I handed to Ricardo a beautifully bound Spanish Bible and a gospel tract with a hundred dollars tucked inside, along with my heartfelt words, "Que Dios le bendiga."

We were grateful not only for the return of the camera but also for the powerful lesson the situation provided us to better understand atomic faith—the force that connects Heaven to Earth. This event became a defining memory for our family. We call the lesson of faith "pray it back."

To this day, our children still talk about the camera miracle in Mexico. The supernatural experience is part of our family's testimony of atomic faith. We had seen the power of faith, reminding us again that nothing—nothing—is impossible with God.

Mark 11:22–26 says that if we don't doubt in our hearts but believe that what we speak in faith will be done, we *will* receive it. That truth is not just about hope or belief; it's about

- *agreeing* with God,
- *activating* faith through our words and actions, and
- *believing* that God always hears and answers our prayers.

Looking back, I realized that the camera lesson of faith was preparation for far greater challenges ahead. The experience strengthened our faith, reminding us that God sees everything—even what may seem lost to us.

The recovered camera experience laid this foundation:

Nothing is too small for God.

He wants to be involved in every detail of our lives, not just the major things but even the smallest. I believe that's why He tells us in Philippians 4:6 not to worry about anything but pray about *everything*. Little or big, God wants us to utilize the principles of faith to daily live an abundant life.

Great Faith Activated

Understanding and using authority in Jesus is part of being successful in the faith journey. Let's look at the authority described in Matthew 8:5–10.

> When Jesus had entered Capernaum, a centurion came to Him, pleading with Him, saying, "Lord, my servant is lying at home paralyzed, dreadfully tormented."
>
> And Jesus said to him, "I will come and heal him."

The centurion answered and said, "Lord, I am not worthy that You should come under my roof. But only speak a word, and my servant will be healed. For I also am a man under authority, having soldiers under me. And I say to this one, 'Go,' and he goes; and to another, 'Come,' and he comes; and to my servant, 'Do this,' and he does it."

When Jesus heard it, He marveled, and said to those who followed, "Assuredly, I say to you, I have not found such great faith, not even in Israel!"

Notice the key phrase Jesus used: "great faith." The centurion recognized God's authority in Jesus and the power that comes from His *rhĕma* word.

How was the power of that *great faith* activated? Not by simply believing but by *doing* something. Although believers in Jesus have God's authority and power available to us, we're still required to take action by faith in what we believe.

The centurion acknowledged that he understood how authority works; he was under authority and had soldiers under his authority. Likely, he was a commander of a hundred Roman military legionaries. The man gave examples of how he directed his men: "I say to this one, 'Go,' and he goes; and to another, 'Come,' and he comes."

Authority and Faith

The centurion understood what response was required: *action*. In like manner, God has given His authority to every believer in Jesus. And as Jesus did, we must exercise our authority by utilizing *faith in action.*

Can we expect anything to become reality by sitting in an office and simply thinking about it? Or believe in something we want to change without taking action that helps to bring it about? In the same way, we must *use* faith to take possession of the object of our belief. We must *do* something to activate the authority of God's power in us.

Exercise your God-given authority by taking action in agreement with what you believe.

Without exercising your authority from God, that power will not do you any good. The military man recognized that Jesus spoke with authority and that Jesus was representing God on Earth.

Jesus is the Son of God, so how else could He have carried such authority that miraculously changed things? The blind gained sight, the lame walked, the sick were healed, and the poor received provision.

In response to the soldier's request, Jesus said, "I will come and heal him."

The soldier answered, "Lord, I am not worthy that You should come under my roof. But only speak a word, and my servant will be healed."

In faith action, the man essentially conveyed to Jesus,

> "You don't need to physically come to my house for my servant to be healed. Just speak the word [an action of authority]. I'm a military man under authority

who understands how the chain of command works [Heaven linking to Earth]. If you simply *speak* the word, because of Your authority, I know [believe] that my servant will be healed. I know this because when I tell a soldier to do something, he goes and does it, and when I tell him to come, he comes." (author paraphrase)

Isn't it interesting that the man, whom Jesus said had *great faith*, understood that taking action by *speaking* in agreement with his belief could move people from one place to another and change circumstances?

Coupling our authority in Jesus with our atomic faith in action creates a bridge between Heaven's power and Earth—power that manifests something visible from the invisible spiritual dimension.

Just as the military officer understood authority in rank, he trusted the authority and spoken words of Jesus—the Commander of Heaven and Earth. In other words, if Jesus said the healing was done, it was done. Jesus acknowledged the soldier's faith: "I have not found such *great faith*, not even in Israel!"

Seeking to know God's will and seeking His righteousness through belief in Jesus are key components to having effective faith. Then we add the authority of Jesus in us and take action based on what we believe in our hearts. These combined aspects of faith form the foundation of atomic faith.

The Story of the Lost Earring

Celebrating a special wedding anniversary, Paula and I embarked on a memorable cruise from the Port of Los Angeles. We sailed aboard the *Sapphire Princess*, a grand vessel carrying about 2,600 passengers. The voyage was a fourteen-day cruise from Southern California to the Hawaiian Islands, where we had decades earlier celebrated our honeymoon.

Paula had packed a pair of earrings that held deep sentimental value. They were a cherished gift from her mother when Paula became a princess in the Tournament of Roses Court in 1971. The earrings were precious to Paula—and, by extension, to me.

The giant cruise ship was a bustling environment of thousands of passengers. Many lined up for portraits on the first night, a cruise tradition. Paula wore her special earrings for the occasion. Afterward, we enjoyed an elegant dinner followed by a comedy show.

When we returned to our room, Paula realized one of her earrings was missing.

We had been on multiple decks and visited several venues—dining room, grand staircase, theater, outside deck, elevators, and restrooms. The earring could be just about anywhere on the massive ship.

Immediately, we searched our cabin to no avail. But Paula didn't give up. In response, she began praying with determination and confidence that the earring would return. I did my best to help, agreeing with her in prayer and checking at the lost and found.

While we searched persistently, Paula remained calm and steadfast in faith. As the trip moved forward and we walked through the ship, enjoying outings, the shows, and dining in various restaurants, Paula continually scanned the ground for the earring while thanking God for bringing back her precious possession.

With over 2,500 passengers and countless areas to search, the odds of recovering the earring were certainly slim. It was small and dangly, a black cut stone in a gold setting, not easy to spot on the vast black and floral carpeting throughout the ship.

Paula rechecked every location she remembered visiting the first night, searching floors and chairs where we'd been. Certain that God would answer her prayers, she also asked the dining staff, "Has an earring been found?" With expectation, she continued to thank God throughout the cruise.

At one point, she asked herself, "Do I want to spend this cruise looking down the entire time? No. But I will. The earring is precious to me, and God has given me the tools to reclaim it."

Whenever Paula takes a stand of faith, she's like a dog with a bone. We'd already learned to "pray it back."

Day after day, Paula thanked God for bringing her earring back. She knew it was hers to reclaim, so she boldly asked God for its return in Jesus's name and with His authority. At the same time, she never stopped searching, fully expecting to find it, and I checked the lost and found daily. We understood that we were partners with God in this recovery effort.

The final morning of the fourteen-day cruise arrived, and still no earring. Nevertheless, Paula's faith remained unchanged.

I visited the lost and found one last time, but again, no earring.

We packed our luggage, gave the room another thorough search, and joined the thousands of passengers heading toward the ship's exit, an area I didn't remember us ever being in.

The passageway was very wide and brimming with people and luggage. Though we were heading out of the ship for good, and among thousands of shuffling feet, our eyes still diligently scanned the carpet for the small piece of jewelry. We were also trying not to let our search overshadow the joy of our cruise, knowing we only had minutes before we'd exit.

As we neared the final yards of the broad hallway, a glint on the carpet caught Paula's eye. She bent down, holding her breath. *Could this be it?*

Directly in her path of the heavily-trafficked space lay a small piece of jewelry. Her missing earring!

Against all odds, the earring had reappeared—at the last possible moment.

How had it gotten here?!

Inspecting it in awe, we found that only the back post was bent. Otherwise, the earring was in perfect condition!

Paula's steadfast faith had been rewarded.

Musing aloud with wonder over the odds, I asked her, "Why do you think no one else saw it and picked it up?"

Her response was simple. "It was difficult to see—but I was expecting to find it. No one else was."

Throughout the cruise, Paula had adhered to a guiding Scripture: "Do not turn to the right or to the left" (Proverbs 4:27). And in the end, she found the earring exactly where she had kept her focus—directly in front of her, in the middle of the hallway, just steps before we exited the ship.

That experience was another powerful reminder that what may seem small or insignificant to others can be of great value to us and, by extension, to God. Paula's determination, anchored in faith, demonstrated that even the most unlikely prayers can be answered in the most unexpected ways. Her earring, a seemingly trivial object, became a testament to the strength of faith and the rewards of unwavering belief in God's goodness.

> "Whatever you ask in My name, that I will do, that the Father may be glorified in the Son. If you ask anything in My name, I will do it." – John 14:13–14

The Lifestyle of an Abundant Life

The value we place on what we pray for is significant to God. Many people struggle to have faith for small things, but if it matters to us, it matters to the Lord. Nothing is too small or too big for God. He wants to be involved in every aspect of your life and see you walk in the lifestyle He designed for His children.

God has given us the option to live that lifestyle—the abundant life Jesus promised. But that doesn't happen by itself. We bring abundant life into reality according to what we believe and by our faith in action.

Jesus leads us step by step, taking us as far as our faith allows. He will not move beyond the boundaries of our faith, but He strengthens our faith through the small challenges, much like exercising a muscle.

If we cannot have faith in the little things, how can we expect to have faith for the bigger ones?

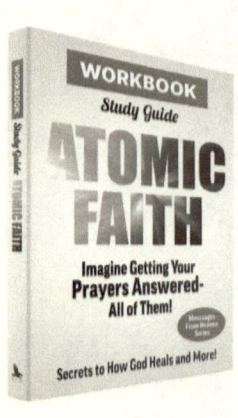

Chapter 13

PRAY IT BACK
THE STORY OF THE STOLEN TRUCK

"Have faith in God. For assuredly, I say to you,
whoever says to this mountain, 'Be removed
and be cast into the sea,' and does not doubt in
his heart, but believes that those things he says
will be done, he will have whatever he says."
— Mark 11:22–23

WE ALL FACE SETBACKS IN LIFE. When these happen, the Bible tells us to "have faith in God." What is lost or taken can be restored if we believe God's promises and pray with faith. Our family experienced this firsthand with dozens and dozens of items, such as the missing camera and earring that miraculously returned.

This earthly life is no match for the power of our faith rooted in the Word of God. When we're spiritually reborn, we inherit the supernatural tools of Heaven. But to live as God intended, we must learn to use these tools effectively.

Accurately understanding God's Word helps us unlock His will for each situation. By knowing His will, we can discern which battles to fight and how to face them with atomic faith.

In 1 Samuel 30, David and his men returned to their camp after a battle only to find it invaded. The enemy had taken their wives, children, and livestock. In that painful moment of harsh discovery and profound loss, "David *strengthened himself* in the Lord his God" (v. 6, author emphasis). His action demonstrates the essential first step toward recovery and forward direction: seeking the Lord for strength and comfort.

Many of David's men were angry over the loss, blaming him for taking them away to fight, leaving their families unprotected. Amid their turmoil and grief, David's second step in response stands out in verse eight: "David inquired of the Lord, saying, 'Shall I pursue this troop? Shall I overtake them?'"

And God answered him, "Pursue, for you shall surely overtake them and without fail recover all."

With that powerful *rhéma* word of authority and promise from God, David and his men pursued the enemy with faith and expectation. The result? They recovered all that was stolen from them—their wives, children, and livestock—without a single loss.

By learning what God has done in other situations, as with David's, we find guidance for how to respond when we experience a loss.

The Story of the Stolen Truck

Our daughter, Kara, was twenty-three when she faced a huge loss. She was living in a gated apartment complex in Orange County, California. Her primary employment was supervising at a group home for abused and neglected boys ages nine to seventeen. She also worked part-time, professionally installing blinds and window coverings for a company we owned.

Kara's vehicle was a 1994 Chevy Silverado pickup, which she loved. The truck was well-used but in decent condition. It provided her with an essential work vehicle, which she had stocked with an array of professional tools.

Humorously, she'd named the truck "Gremlin" because items often mysteriously disappeared, to later reappear.

Late one night, Kara had driven home, entered the gates of her highly secured apartment complex, and, as usual, parked Gremlin in her designated parking space. She was about to emerge from the vehicle when she experienced an unusual prompting to pray for her truck's protection. Though puzzled by the out-of-the-blue prodding, she obeyed. She placed her hands on the dashboard and prayed for Gremlin's safety.

The next morning, Kara headed to her truck and was stunned to find Gremlin missing! Her shock gave way to confusion, and she wandered the parking lot, searching for her truck. She hoped she had somehow mistakenly parked elsewhere in the previous night's late hour.

But Gremlin was nowhere to be found.

As the knot in Kara's stomach grew, she faced the realization that her truck had been stolen.

Feeling numb with shock, she called us. We prayed with her that Gremlin would be found and returned.

Kara then contacted the police, who arrived quickly to take a report. The officers, though kind, did not offer any hope. Officer Jessica in particular was candid. "Trucks like yours are often stolen. For as long as I've been an officer, I've heard of very few ever recovered, especially given our proximity to the Mexican border," she added.

Kara's heart plummeted further.

"Most stolen vehicles," the officer continued, "are either parted out in local illegal chop shops or sent across the border for resale." She urged Kara to temper her expectations and lean on her insurance.

Kara called her insurance company, only to be hit with further discouraging news. "If your truck isn't recovered within thirty days, it'll be considered totaled."

The agent's next blow was the amount the insurance would pay, leaving Kara with a huge balance owed on her truck loan: $10,200. Her frustration quickly turned to anger.

Then she remembered the prompting she'd had the previous night to pray over Gremlin. Suddenly, that spiritual urging held deeper significance, leading Kara to question God. *Why would You prompt me to pray for the truck's protection only for it to be stolen? What's going on?*

Except for Paula and me, everyone Kara told about the theft responded similarly: "It's gone. You'll never see your truck again. You might as well start shopping for a new one."

During that discouraging and puzzling time, Kara and Paula had a pivotal conversation. Paula reminded her of the many times God had intervened in our family's numerous and varied losses. "He returned stolen airplanes, stolen cameras, lost wallets holding lots of cash . . . even miraculous healings! God restored them by the supernatural power of our faith, exactly as Jesus taught.

"Sweetheart, view this challenge as an opportunity to exercise your faith and spiritual authority," Paula encouraged. "Remember David's victories over the lion and the bear? And the confidence those victories gave him to face and defeat Goliath?" Then she gently reminded Kara of God's timing. "God graciously prompted you to pray *before* Gremlin was stolen."

> God has the answer to every need and question. He patiently waits for you to show faith in your choices. When faith is added to your prayers, God will fulfill your requests.
>
> Jesus described that relationship with Him as being yoked with Him—working together in every situation.
>
> > "Come to Me, all you who labor and are heavy laden, and I will give you rest. Take My yoke upon you and learn from Me, for I am gentle and lowly in heart, and you will find rest for your souls. For My yoke is easy and My burden is light." — Matthew 11:28–30

For about three days, Kara wrestled with frustration and questions. However, she ultimately came to a decisive commitment to approach the stolen truck God's way, using atomic faith.

Rather than staying angry at the enemy for stealing the truck, Kara decided to "get even" with satan. She flatly refused to accept the prognosis from the police, the insurance company, and her friends. She chose to take a firm stand of faith.

> From my decades of experience with God, I've learned that when I think I'm waiting on Him, it's often the other way around—God is waiting on me. He's waiting for me to ask Him specifically, and with gratitude, expectation, and unwavering faith. In other words, He's waiting on me to use atomic faith.

When you think you're waiting on God, it's often the other way around—God is waiting on you.

After the pivotal talk with her mother, Kara transformed into a strong faith warrior. She thanked the Lord in faith for bringing Gremlin back to her, and she spoke to everyone, including Officer Jessica, about her faith to "pray it back." She'd say, "God will bring my truck back. You'll see!"

As Kara continued to deal with the same insurance agent and Officer Jessica, she fervently continued thanking the Lord for Gremlin's return, claiming ownership of her truck in the spiritual realm.

She knew from the Bible that as a child of God, she had the authority of *Jesus* on her side! Empowered by this perspective, Kara declared spiritual war. Three times a day, she prayed with atomic faith, taking inspiration from the many challenges Daniel (of the Old Testament) had fought and won by faith.

Kara's faith grew as she refused to give in to doubt. Even as her friends expressed concern for her emotional state, and the insurance agent and Officer Jessica utterly dismissed her optimism, Kara remained resolute in her belief that Gremlin would be found and returned. Repeatedly, she proclaimed to doubters, "God will bring my truck back. You'll see!"

Twenty-six days after the theft, Kara received the expected call from an excited Officer Jessica. "I can't believe this, but . . . your truck has been found, just 2.4 miles from your apartment."

Kara was ecstatic. She praised God for answering her prayers, honoring her faith, and bringing victory out of loss.

The officer picked up Kara at her apartment and drove her to the junkyard where the truck had been discovered.

At first sight of her truck, Kara was astonished. "That's not my truck!" Gremlin had been stripped of its shell and interior and gutted for numerous parts. Nonetheless, the vehicle was undeniably Gremlin—the same color, VIN, and even the familiar dent. Small, insignificant, but personal items in the cup holder also confirmed the truck was hers. But Gremlin had been sorely ravaged.

Still, Kara was full of joy over her vindicated faith and God's incredible work on her behalf. Her faith had bridged God's power from Heaven to Earth, making a way where there seemed no way (Isaiah 43:16–19). She beamed at Officer Jessica and, pointing a finger at her, said, "I told you God would bring it back!"

The officer, though stunned by the outcome, acknowledged it was the first miracle she'd ever witnessed.

Kara used the moment to share more about her relationship with God. "As a child of God, I have spiritual authority over my possessions. If God can do this for me," she said confidently, "imagine what He can do for you."

Immediately, a favorite Scripture came to Kara's mind, and she realized she had lived out its truth in this battle of her faith.

> "Whatever you ask in My name, that I will do, that the Father may be glorified in the Son. If you ask anything in My name, I will do it." — John 14:13–14

Kara had taken God's way against a tide of opposing opinions. In her fight of faith, God proved His Word, will, promises, power, and faithfulness. In the process, Kara discovered the benefits of using atomic faith.

Kara couldn't resist sharing her victory with anyone who'd listen. Her awe of God and the power of her faith yoked with Jesus was overflowing.

> Whatever is born of God overcomes the world. And this is the victory that has overcome the world—our faith. — 1 John 5:4

When Kara reported the truck's recovery to her insurance company, the familiar agent was shocked and excited. "We'll arrange to restore the truck—since it was found within the thirty-day window."

Within ten days, Gremlin was returned to Kara—in stunningly pristine condition. Every missing part had been replaced, brand-new. Gremlin returned in far better condition than when it was stolen. It was nicer than when Kara had bought it. New upholstery, a new steering wheel, a new dashboard, a new interior liner, the dent fixed, and the body completely repainted. Kara's faithful prayers had been answered "exceedingly abundantly above all that" she could "ask or think, according to the power that works in us" (Ephesians 3:20).

Officer Jessica accompanied Kara to pick up the newly restored truck. The officer had difficulty admitting what an unusual and amazing experience it was to find the stolen vehicle, let alone see the entire event turn out so perfectly.

Kara again took the opportunity to share her insights with the officer. "Faith and spiritual authority brought my truck back. When you own something," she explained, "you have authority over it. God gave us promises we can stand on about that authority. And if we act in faith on His promises, He'll answer according to our faith."

Kara renamed her restored truck "Faith" in honor of the journey she and her vehicle had been through. She shared her story with many friends. As a result, they were inspired to pray for the recovery of their lost items—from keys to purses to electronics—which brought about numerous personal testimonies.

> Jesus said, "Whatever things you ask in prayer, believing, you will receive." — Matthew 21:22

Kara reflected that God had used the theft to teach her and others valuable lessons about hope, belief, faith, and spiritual authority. She shared, "I realized God was guiding me to do something unusual by prompting me to pray for my truck before it was stolen.

Kara later shared, "Growing up, I witnessed in my family many 'pray it back' victories. Faith wasn't just something we believed in; faith was something we actively practiced. Even though I was young when my truck was stolen, I knew it wasn't right to depend on someone else's belief. The truck was mine, and I had authority over it. It was up to me to take the lead and pray it back with atomic faith."

Kara often encourages others to take spiritual authority over their possessions and lives, reminding them of Jesus's direction, "Have faith in God" (Mark 11:22), and His promise, "If you ask anything in My name, I will do it" (John 14:14).

If Jesus is your Savior and Lord, you have the authority of His name to change your circumstances.

Since that Gremlin-turned-Faith experience, Kara became what she calls a "pray it back advocate."

If you haven't used faith in action, *atomic faith*, a great start is to *pray back* whatever you've lost. But your belief and faith must be unwavering.

Take to heart this truth as a believer in Jesus: Your possessions, including your physical body, health, and healing, are under your spiritual authority. You can use that authority in agreement with the name of Jesus to *fight in faith* for the safe return or restoration of whatever you've lost.

The Authority of Jesus's Name

An important aspect of faith is understanding the authority of Jesus's name and all that His name stands for.

From the time Jesus ascended from Earth into Heaven, His followers became His earthly representatives. All followers of the Lord have access to the power of His authority. The same power and authority Jesus used to heal the sick, cast out demons, and raise the dead is available to those who are His so they may overcome the enemy and bring glory to God.

> "Behold, I give you the authority to trample on serpents and scorpions, and over all the power of the enemy, and nothing shall by any means hurt you."
> — Luke 10:19

In today's world, many who claim Jesus have quit taking the Bible literally. Countless have reduced their view of God's Word to "inspirational literature" and seldom apply the living, active Word (Hebrews 4:12) to their daily lives. Yet Jesus lived each day according to God's Word and will.

The Confidence of Knowing What Is True

Keeping Scripture in context with its surrounding related passages is *essential* to knowing and having confidence in the truth of God's Word! Many followers of Jesus take single verses or short passages out of context, which weakens the impact of God's principles. This misuse has led many to stop viewing God's Word as literal and alive.

There is great supernatural power in believing God and His Word literally and in context. God meant what He said and said what He meant.

In this chapter, we saw joy overflow as our daughter's faith was powerfully justified through God's incredible work. By acting on what she believed, her faith bridged the gap between Heaven and Earth, creating a way where there seemed to be none (Isaiah 43:16–19).

The stunned police officer recognized the miracle, which provided Kara an opening to share her faith: God answers the prayers of His children and gives us spiritual authority over our possessions and circumstances. As she had said to the officer, "If God can do this for me, imagine what He can do for you."

Should we pray for everything to be restored to us? Is this always how God works, or does He sometimes choose a different, yet equally wonderful, approach? We'll explore these questions in detail in the Atomic Faith Workbook and illustrate the principals through a true story in Chapter 17, "Reaping the Miraculous."

Chapter 14

THE BREAKING POINT OF FAITH
THE STORY OF A MIRACLE OVER MIGRAINES

Faith comes by hearing, and
hearing by the word of God.
— Romans 10:17

GOD WORKS WITH EACH OF US ON AN INDIVIDUAL BASIS. He guides and directs our steps as we allow. When we ask God for help, He answers our prayers personally and specifically according to our faith.

Faith is like a muscle; it must be developed to grow stronger. Our key Scripture, Romans 10:17, provides clear guidance on how to strengthen our faith.

In this verse, the term "word" is the Greek word *rhēma*, as explained in Chapter 2, meaning an utterance or spoken word; a direct, personal communication and understanding from God's Spirit to your heart. Also noted in Chapter 2, *rhéma* emphasizes that a revealed word from God builds faith.

Rhéma is a specific word from God's Spirit to your heart for your situation that ignites your faith to believe.

Rhéma also means a word of divine revelation. God's *rhéma* words are uniquely tailored to you for your specific situation, offering guidance and insight for your journey. A *rhéma* is not generally an audible voice that others or you can hear with physical ears but a spiritual voice or message heard in our hearts or revealed through what we hear from teachings of God's Word.

Understanding the true meaning of *rhéma* is essential to learning how God directs our steps.

On rare occasions, God's *rhéma* may be audible—or at least seem that way. More commonly, *rhéma* is God's Spirit communicating with our spirits.

A *rhéma* experience often occurs through the Holy Spirit's direct interaction with our spirits, or by His Spirit highlighting in us a specific passage of Scripture we're reading.

Remember, when we take action based on God's *rhéma* within us, His supernatural power is unleashed into the situation. God-powered faith, which I call atomic faith, is the kind of faith that works miracles, as described in Mark 9:23: "All things are possible to him who believes."

The following story illustrates what can happen when we shift from our worldly thinking to align with Jesus's teachings. When we activate our faith in response to God's Word, we've ignited *atomic faith* that leads to answered prayers. The illustration below highlights the power of God's *logos* (written) Word and His *rhēma* (spoken) word.

The Story of a Miracle Over Migraines

When I woke up from the three-day coma following the crash, my perspective was entirely changed. Nearly two years later, at age twenty-one, God was continually teaching me as I read the Bible. As I learned something new, I'd put it into action, which exercised my faith muscle.

As I delved deeper into God's *logos* Word, I continued testing His principles in practice. I had started connecting the dots between my supernatural healings and my belief in the powerful truths of Scripture, such as Isaiah 53:5, "By His stripes we are healed."

The miraculous results of believing His Word in hand with taking faith actions is why I began to call the supernatural power *atomic faith*.

Scripture was making clear to me that by the whippings (stripes) Jesus endured on His body, I was already healed—past tense!

This realization completely transformed my thinking.

Jesus had already paid the full price for my healing, and I chose to believe His Word was literally true for me—right then and there. As I practiced atomic faith based on that belief, I actively received the healing Jesus had already secured for me.

As answers to my prayers faithfully materialized, the pattern of His design for faith in action became clearer:

- God had made a promise in His Word.
- I believed what He offered was literal.
- I took action in faith according to my belief and continued to do so until the answers came, however long it took.
- The answers always came.

For example, the traumatic head injuries I had sustained caused severe memory loss. But I discovered that creating mental images for every experience helped me overcome the memory challenges and retain information more easily.

One of the most vivid and transformative images I formed came from Isaiah 53:5. I pictured Jesus on the cross, His blood flowing from His wounds, enduring unimaginable pain for my healing, which was also for your healing and for anyone who firmly believes God's *logos* (written) Word as truth. Jesus paid the price for all of us, every person, and those who take the bold step of atomic faith receive that truth for their specific situation.

Visualizing the scene of Jesus on the cross helped me grasp the reality of Isaiah 53:5 in a deeply personal way. "He was wounded for our transgressions, He was bruised for our iniquities."

The image changed how I approached every challenge, great and small, from that moment on. I understood that Jesus's suffering wasn't only for physical healing but, more importantly, for the full payment of our sins.

During that time, I was trying to get back into my life, which required juggling demanding responsibilities. I had returned to driving eighteen-wheelers (double-trailer truck rigs) for my family's business, working long hours to pay for my flying lessons and college expenses. In addition, I was enduring debilitating migraines, a lingering effect of the severe head trauma I sustained in the crash.

Often while driving my truck, I would be struck with an incapacitating migraine. I would turn to God and pray, "I know I'm healed by the stripes Jesus took on His body for me. Thank You for the healing You've provided."

But despite my prayers, the pain would persist. The only relief I found was taking four extra-strength pain relievers every few hours.

For about a year, I endured frequent, agonizing migraines, and each time, I would declare aloud in prayer, "I am healed!" Yet the pain remained. I couldn't function without the medication I always kept nearby.

Frustration grew in me. I had previously experienced God's miraculous healing multiple times through prayer and effort, so why wasn't I finding the same breakthrough with these migraines? My ankle had been supernaturally restored, my severely injured right eye had improved to near-perfect vision, and my left shoulder was "a miracle," according to Dr. Graham. I knew God's promises were true and that He was faithful, yet no healing from migraines?

What am I doing wrong? Am I missing something? Is there an error in my approach? Is God trying to teach me something more?

Then it hit me. The answer came to mind as clearly as if God were verbally responding: "If you truly believe I've healed you, and you believe My Word is true—*By His stripes, we are healed'*—why are you carrying pain pills on the dashboard of your truck?"

The realization shook me to the core and forced me to confront the inconsistency between my declarations of faith and my actions. That pivotal moment further refined my understanding of how I should live out my trust in God's Word.

A quick moment later was this thought: *I should throw the pills away at the next truck stop.*

For the next two weeks, I continued promising myself I'd throw away the painkillers. But I didn't. Deep down, I didn't believe tossing them would solve my problem. I reasoned that if God was going to heal me, He could whether or not I had the pills within reach. Yet the thought of getting rid of the pills continued to hound me.

One night, as I was driving northbound on Interstate 5 in Southern California, another severe migraine started. By the time I began climbing the mountains of Gorman Pass, the pain was unbearable. I was near my breaking point. The intensity had grown so severe that one eye involuntarily closed, and I could barely think. My dependency on the pills was clear, though they only dampened the pain.

I'd had enough!

I yelled, "God! This is NOT right! Please help me!"

Again, amid my struggle, His gentle voice whispered in me, "Dale, if you truly believe My Word, let go of the pills."

Though His words struck me, my thoughts quickly shifted back to the reality of my driving. I was a professional truck driver, yet now dangerous on the interstate, controlling

80,000 pounds of rig and cargo. I could barely see or think and desperately needed to pull off the road.

Approaching the next off-ramp—two miles, one mile, a half mile . . .—I levered the blinker on, signaling my exit.

"Who do you trust?" God asked within me. "Do you believe My Word, or is your trust in the pills?"

In a matter of seconds, and in excruciating pain, I did the unthinkable. Flicking off the blinker, I kept rolling and passed the off-ramp, one eye still closed. I screamed in agony and frustration, "God, I trust You! But help me!"

The pain was overwhelming, eclipsing every other concern. I no longer cared about the truck, the cargo, or the tight schedule; I was consumed by the relentless throbbing in my body.

A prompting caused me to think a seemingly impossible thought. I grabbed the pills and opened my window. Hesitating, I glanced at the source of my relief and questioned, *Do I dare?* Instantly the image of Jesus's suffering for me flashed in my mind. Quickly gauging no left-hand traffic, I violently threw the bottle out the window.

With God as my witness, what I'm about to tell you is entirely true. In that very moment—the exact millisecond the bottle left my hand—the migraine vanished. All the pain, every bit, disappeared instantly. Gone!

That was fifty-five years ago, and I haven't had a migraine since.

At that time, I was still young in hearing God's voice (*rhéma*) and learning His ways. Now much older, wiser, and practiced, I'm confident in His answers and His infallible Word.

>**Important Note:** I want to be very clear; I am not suggesting you throw your medications away! As I stated at the onset of this chapter, God works with each of us individually and often in unique ways. He's also gentle and patient, working with His children from our baby steps forward. He's aware that new believers are more prone to falling. Not "failing" but simply falling as we learn to walk with Him.

>Over the years, I've learned a great deal about falling and getting back up.

I was pursuing God's best for me. In my heart, I wanted all of Him and all that He offered, including the seemingly impossible. By "impossibly" surviving a horrific, fatal airplane crash, I knew I was a living miracle. No doubt.

As I pressed into the Lord, reading His Word, listening for His voice within me, and strengthening my faith muscle, He challenged me further. God's Spirit urged me to let go of my earthly dependencies and place my entire faith in Him and His Word. His *rhēma* and *logos* words were rooting deeper in my heart.

God is a healing God.
He wants you well!

I'm grateful to have come to understand these truths:

- Faith is a profoundly powerful spiritual force.
- Patience—being steadfast and persevering—is equally potent in the spiritual realm.
- Faith and patience working together can indeed move mountains.

If we plant the living Word of God in the soil of our hearts, listen with spiritual ears to His voice within us, and take action in faith, atomic power will burst forth, and the result will be answered prayer.

Faith Is Acting On What You Believe

You won't find that definition of faith in dictionaries, so using faith as a verb takes some getting used to.

We've seen in historical stories that Heaven's version of faith is the opposite of this world's way of thinking. Why is that not surprising? Satan is at work, he's the god of this world, and he's strategically robbing God's people of spiritual power through false doctrines and compromised teaching.

God's powerful truths are not found in man's watered-down, compromised doctrines and paraphrased Bibles. Earthly wisdom is foolishness to God:

> If anyone among you seems to be wise in this age, let him become a fool that he may become wise. For the wisdom of this world is foolishness with God. For it is written, "He catches the wise in their own craftiness"; and again, "The Lord knows the thoughts of the wise, that they are futile."
> — 1 Corinthians 3:18–20

In addition, today's corporate church structure has been largely robbed of solid biblical truth that teaches us how to connect with God's power. Satan fears Jesus and thereby works diligently to reduce and try to eliminate Jesus's power, His supremacy, and His authority.

You may be going through this book because you want your life to operate better. Possibly, you've been hoping for ways to improve or solve some problems you're facing. That's all good. But in *Atomic Faith*, you're discovering the truth of God's undiluted, uncompromised Word, which hopefully you are discovering is more powerful than you have previously understood.

God's written Word teaches us how to tap into His power: the miracle-working power Jesus demonstrated—the power of faith in action that ignites the power that brings Heaven to Earth.

Faith is not simply believing. Faith is acting on what you believe.

Let's remember, the Bible says that "faith without works is dead" (James 2:26). If that's true, isn't the opposite also true? Active faith is alive with the power of God!

Believing without *taking action* is lifeless, and no power can be released from what is lifeless. So, as necessary as belief is, atomic faith cannot be released to bring about answer prayers without putting it into action.

Again . . . We Don't Know What We Don't Know

Many people *think* they know what faith is. I've met a lot of folks who *think* they're walking by faith every day.

However, if we were to observe their day-to-day living, we'd see a universal problem of humanity: People do not know what they don't know!

As I've traveled the globe for many decades, I've seen this continual problem. However, the greater problem is when people think they *do* know what they don't. Such thinkers are usually unteachable because they *think* they already know what they don't. That's often the case when an individual has spent decades under inaccurate teaching.

When a person has been mistaught or assumed a truth based on incorrect teaching, they are usually not open to a different idea. We're all susceptible to this trap. That's the very reason we must continually read the Bible. As we do, the Holy Spirit opens our eyes to the conflicts between what we believe and what His Word says.

Scripture challenges us to continually renew our minds to God's way of thinking and doing. Humanity is constantly being programmed with beliefs that support the worldview and system, usually contrary to God's view and His ways.

> Do not be conformed to this world, but be transformed by the renewing of your mind.
> — Romans 12:2

Adopting a new way of thinking isn't easy. However, the goal of this book is to guide you in renewing your mind to think the way God thinks, as we've seen in Scripture.

Each time I stepped out in faith on the *rhēma* word of God, my prayers were answered, and the impossible became possible. Mountains were moved.

Remember, faith is acting on what you believe.

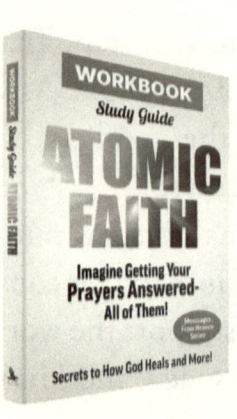

Chapter 15

FIGHTING THE GOOD FIGHT OF FAITH
THE GEORGE FOREMAN STORY

> "I say to you, whatever things you ask
> when you pray, believe that you receive
> them, and you will have them."
> — Mark 11:24

THE INVISIBLE ASPECT OF GOD'S WAYS IS THE OPPOSITE OF HOW THE WORLD FUNCTIONS AND THINKS. The world says, "I'll believe it when I see it." But since the Bible says, "Faith is the evidence of things not seen" (Hebrews 11:1), the truth is, "You'll see it when you believe it."

Jesus said, "Blessed are those who have not seen and yet have believed" (John 20:29). Therefore, if we want to understand how to have our prayers answered, we'll need to renew our minds to agree with God and His way. What is His way?

You'll see it when you believe it.

From cover to cover in the Bible, we see God at work through His *logos* and *rhéma* words. With faith, we believe His words and His ways are true, whether written or spoken, visible to us or invisible.

Consider Hebrews 11:3, "By faith we understand that the worlds were framed by the [*rhéma*] word of God, so that the things which are seen were not made of things which are visible."

In other words, "By Him all things were created that are in Heaven and that are on earth, visible and invisible, whether thrones or dominions or principalities or powers. All things were created through Him and for Him" (Colossians 1:16).

The ultimate outcome of our faith is a visible realization. Before the answer becomes visible, it's invisible but just as real as when it becomes visible. To keep the answer alive until it becomes visible, patience is needed. Why? Letting go of our faith at any time during the waiting phase allows doubt and unbelief to creep in and abort the answer.

> Knowing that the testing of your faith produces patience . . . let patience have its perfect work, that you may be perfect and complete, lacking nothing.
> — James 1:3–4

The Power Twins: Faith and Patience

Faith and patience go hand in hand. I often call them "the power twins" because both are essential for breakthroughs in answered prayer. Faith and patience combined will bring the invisible to the visible.

Have you ever seen a welder cut through a plate of steel? The acetylene torch blasts a flame so hot and powerful that it can slice through thick steel. But if the welder continually moves the torch, the steel will only be warmed. To cut through it, the welder not only needs the force and power of the torch but also *focus*: The torch must be held steady in one spot to achieve a breakthrough.

In the same way, the forces of faith and patience working together bring God's supernatural power from Heaven to Earth in answered prayer. Not just sometimes, but every time.

The George Foreman Story: The Making of a Champion—Twice

George Foreman's story is one of grit, faith, and the ultimate comeback—one that defied all odds. As this book, *Atomic Faith*, neared publication, I received word that brother George Foreman had passed into Heaven. Big George exemplified what it means to walk by faith, not by sight. He finished his race with boldness and unwavering faith. He didn't merely speak about faith; he lived it, inspiring others to do the same. You may remember him proclaiming to millions, "Jesus came alive in me!"[9] Though he will be missed, we rejoice that George is now *truly* alive with his Lord and Savior, Jesus.

Before I tell you about George Foreman's incredible history, I want to make one thing clear: This isn't just a boxing story. It's about how God took an old, worn-out boxer and led him back to the top for a reason far beyond personal glory. George's story honors the Lord of Glory, and I hope it brings hope and encouragement to you.

George Foreman was a professional boxer who rose to fame as one of the hardest-hitting punchers in boxing history. He became the world heavyweight champion when he knocked out none other than "Smokin'" Joe Frazier, an exceptionally powerful opponent.

George, also known as "Big George" for his towering presence in and out of the ring, was not only one of the most successful boxers of all time but also an outstanding entrepreneur and author. He became widely known for the George Foreman grill, a product sold worldwide for decades.

After achieving the world championship, George had an extraordinary spiritual encounter, which I'll share in detail a bit later. From that transformative experience, he became a powerful, unique minister of the gospel of Jesus Christ. However, prior, his life was far from conventional.

George's early years tell the story of a troubled childhood in a difficult location in America. "I was always out during the night mugging people," George confessed.[10] For him, mugging seemed like the only way to get ahead. "I didn't know anything about anything except being hungry," he said, reflecting his harsh reality.[11]

Despite those early challenges, George found his way to boxing. He was only nineteen when he won the Olympic gold medal in the heavyweight division. Five years later, he earned the world heavyweight championship—a moment I was fortunate to witness live from the second row. An unforgettable event.

A year later, George was famously defeated by Muhammad Ali in the "Rumble in the Jungle" (which I was also fortunate to see in person). Ali introduced his "rope-a-dope" strategy during that historic fight, wearing George down before Ali delivered the knockout blow. George later admitted he'd harbored a deep hatred for Ali long after.

Although he continued fighting in the futile hope of reclaiming his title, Foreman became increasingly frustrated and angry, his deep hatred for Ali growing. In a brutal match against Jimmy Young, George was defeated again and suffered severe injuries. Afterward, in his dressing room, he described having a life-altering experience and later claimed he had briefly died. He described falling "into a deep dark nothing, just like in a sea. All I can remember is this hopelessness, this nothing, and a horrible smell that went along with this nothing. Like a big dump yard of nothing.[12]

"I knew I was dead, and this wasn't heaven. I was terrified, knowing I had no way out. Sorrow beyond description engulfed my soul, more than anyone could ever imagine. If you multiplied every disturbing and frightening thought that you've ever had during your entire life, that wouldn't come close to the panic I felt. . . . I screamed with every ounce of strength in me, 'I don't care if this *is* death. I still believe there's a God!'"[13]

That's when George realized something deeper: Simply believing there's a God is not enough. Even satan and all the demons of hell know there is a God.

In that moment of despair, George had a vision of Jesus Christ with blood running down from His head. This was a heart-changing moment for George.

"Instantly, what seemed to be like a gigantic hand reached down and snatched me out of the terrifying place. Immediately I was back inside my body in the dressing room."[14]

When George returned to consciousness in his dressing room, he was a completely changed man. He began shouting to everyone around him, "Jesus Christ has come alive in me!"[15]

Those around him were worried he might be delirious from the brutal match. "All I want people to understand is . . . I found God, I found out about Jesus Christ."[16]

George Foreman was changed from the inside out. He realized that life without God had left him empty. "It doesn't matter what your own worst moment is. Storms of all kinds rage through our lives, and sometimes they can take everything from us. But if you have faith, your own worst moment can become your best."[17]

Foreman hung up his boxing gloves and followed Jesus into ministry, serving as a pastor. He devoted his life to spreading the gospel and sharing his story of redemption and transformation. Here are just a few of the many wise thoughts George shared since his powerful transformation of heart and mind:

- "Sometimes God gives instructions that go against conventional wisdom, such as treating people kindly when they're hateful. Who really wants to do that? Instructions like that may not always make sense, so that's why I need to trust and obey the One who inspired them."[18]
- "I'm working for the Lord. . . . And even though the Lord's pay often isn't very high, His retirement program is."[19]
- "Excellence isn't achieved without inspiration and perspiration. You've got to have both."[20]
- "Read the Bible; it is your roadmap through life."[21]

George Foreman's story is one of extraordinary transformation—a testament to the power of redemption, hope, belief, and faith.

While his name will forever be linked to boxing greatness and a popular grill, George Foreman's legacy as a follower of Jesus Christ and preacher of the gospel was, to him, the most significant chapter of his life. He stated, "Don't let any opportunity lead you away from serving God. That's a price that's too high to pay."[22]

George found immense joy in the work he was doing for Jesus. He loved seeing lives changed and being part of something bigger than himself—eternal work. However, he had a persistent nagging feeling; something was calling him back to boxing—back into the ring.

With his prime years far behind him, everyone knew his days in the ring were over. George agreed and thought he had accepted that. He was forty-five, his body slower and his reflexes not as quick. Yet he felt God was calling him back into boxing. He knew God always had a plan. George could no longer ignore God's still, small voice (*rhēma*) persisting inside him. He began to believe that a comeback wasn't just about boxing; it was about fulfilling a greater purpose that would glorify God.

So Foreman resumed serious training, starting with the basics. He could barely keep up and complained that his body ached in ways he hadn't experienced in decades. But George stayed committed. Though he likely wondered what God was up to, he kept training in faith.

The road back wasn't easy, but it held a greater purpose that pushed him forward in the ring and in faith. As with any faith journey, doubts assaulted him from every angle. Most people in the boxing world essentially told George, "You're too old! You can't compete with younger, faster, and stronger fighters." Logically, such statements were true.

Once the media learned of Foreman's comeback decision, they were ruthless. Every headline referenced his return, and the articles emphasized he didn't stand a chance.

But there was God . . . and George believed God was calling him into the seemingly impossible. His response was rooted in believing God's voice and promise: "With God, all things are possible."

With atomic faith in action, Foreman was determined to give boxing everything he had—not for himself but for God's glory, confident that God had a plan. By faith and with rigorous action, George committed to what appeared impossible due to his age and a decade out of training: to again become the world heavyweight champion.

That would be a miracle.

Months became years of training as preparation. For encouragement, George persistently proclaimed in faith, *"I'm going to be the heavyweight champion of the world—again."*[23]

Ultimately, God fulfilled the promise He had placed in George's heart.

Every punch, every step, every hour in the gym was a testament to Foreman's faith, patience, and perseverance. He was committed to showing the world what can happen when we trust in God and refuse to give up, no matter how impossible the odds.

Mark 11:23–24 is said to be one of George's favorite Scripture passages:

> "Assuredly, I say to you, whoever says to this mountain, 'Be removed and be cast into the sea,' and does not doubt in his heart, but believes that those things he says will be done, he will have whatever he says. Therefore I say to you, whatever things you ask when you pray, believe that you receive them, and you will have them."

In 1994, at age forty-five, Foreman reclaimed the world heavyweight title—twenty years after previously earning the championship. He had experienced that God makes way for victories based on His promises. George chose to stand firm on God's promises and take action with atomic faith that he would win against all odds.

Foreman's win wasn't just a boxing comeback victory. His success was a testament to what God will do when His followers act in faith according to His Word.

Earlier, we noted the difference between natural faith, which is limited, and supernatural faith, which knows no bounds. George Foreman demonstrated supernatural faith—a powerful example of atomic faith. Such faith can transform your life and change the world.

Supernatural faith begins with hope, develops into a deep belief in God's Word, and ultimately leads to action based on that belief. Simply put, faith is acting on what you believe.

Foreman regaining the heavyweight title proved to the world that anything is possible.

George said, "There's a living God, . . . and I'm proof of it."[24] His name is Jesus Christ.

A Journey of Supernatural Faith Starts With What Is Not Visible

When you need or desire anything that is not visible, atomic faith is required to realize it. When you're looking to God for answered prayer, remember this: He hears you, and He will respond. But to *receive* the visible answer you desire, there are conditions:

- Praying in agreement with God's will
- Believing what God has promised
- Using faith by acting on what you believe
- Keeping your faith in action with patience until the answer is visible

The answer you have requested is *already formed* in the spiritual realm and *will* become visible in the natural realm by remaining in agreement with God and His will.

As you read through the New Testament, you'll find that the activities of Jesus's apostles imitated His life and ministry. What He demonstrated was what they also did after Jesus filled them with His Holy Spirit.

After Jesus departed Earth, He sent His Holy Spirit (Acts 2) to continue teaching and empowering all who believe in Him to do as He did and more.

> "Most assuredly, I say to you, he who believes in Me, the works that I do he will do also; and greater works than these he will do, because I go to My Father."
> — John 14:12

The Bible also tells us that God does not change: "Jesus Christ is the same yesterday, today, and forever" (Hebrews 13:8).

Isn't it mind-blowing that Jesus told His followers that they would do the same works and even greater than He did?

From my perspective, it's clear that Jesus consistently used faith as a verb to perform the miracles recorded in the New Testament. He encouraged His disciples to do the same, challenging them to perform similar miracles using the same kind of faith. In other words, faith was a verb—acting on what they believed in their hearts.

When you begin to use faith as a verb, grounded in God's Word, your entire perspective on life will shift. Your prayer life, thinking, and daily actions will be wonderfully transformed.

"I say to you, whatever things you ask when you pray, believe that you receive them, and you will have them." — Mark 11:24

The days of simply *hoping* God will answer your prayers can be over. That void and longing become replaced by the *confident expectation* that your prayers are not a matter of "if" but a matter of "when" your answers will become visible.

Chapter 16

THE TINY SEED THAT MOVED MOUNTAINS
THE FLORENCE HAMMILL STORY

Jesus said to them, ". . . If you have faith as a
mustard seed, you will say to this mountain,
'Move from here to there,' and it will move;
and nothing will be impossible for you."
— Matthew 17:20

OVER THE YEARS, I'VE LEARNED THAT WHILE PEOPLE OFTEN KNOW WHAT THEY WANT, THEY SELDOM UNDERSTAND HOW TO GET IT—ESPECIALLY THROUGH PRAYER, ASKING GOD FOR HELP.

For example, someone prays, "God, I need healing," or "Lord, I need a job," or "Please meet our financial needs," or even, "God, I need a spouse. Please provide what I need!"

At first, they pray with hope. But when the answer doesn't come right away, desperation sets in, followed by frustration. Eventually, as the prayer remains unanswered, they give up. The unmet request often leads to questions: *Where is God? Why hasn't He answered? What's going on?*

This pattern continuing can cause a disconnect from God, harming a person's relationship with Him.

Jesus teaches us the how-to answers in the Bible:

> "Ask, and it will be given to you; seek, and you will find; knock, and it will be opened to you. For everyone who asks receives, and he who seeks finds, and to him who knocks it will be opened."
> — Matthew 7:7–8

All Scripture is true. Jesus invites us to bring our needs to God and receive answers. However, as we've learned in previous chapters, there's a key issue that often hinders our prayers from being answered: *unbelief.*

The greatest obstacle to answered prayer is unbelief.

In Matthew 17:19–20, the disciples asked Jesus why they couldn't cast out a demon. He replied, "Because of your unbelief; for assuredly, I say to you, if you have faith as a mustard seed, you will say to this mountain, 'Move from here to there,' and it will move; and nothing will be impossible for you."

Remember, the word *faith* is at times a noun but often a verb. In the verse above, the original Greek word for *faith* is πίστις—translated *pistis*, a noun meaning "belief, trust, confidence."[25] Pistis refers to reliance on God, a strong conviction that He exists, He's trustworthy, and He fulfills His promises.

With that understanding, let's look at the Matthew passage through the lens of its original meaning, as it could read when translated with those definitions in mind:

> The disciples asked Jesus why they couldn't cast out the demon. Jesus replied, "Because of your unbelief. For assuredly, I say to you, if you have *trust, belief, confidence, and a strong conviction that God is trustworthy and fulfills His promises*—with even a tiny, living seed—you can say to this mountain, 'Move from here to there,' and it will move. Nothing will be impossible for you." (author paraphrase)

Jesus's words remind us how powerful the tiniest faith can be. A mustard seed is small, yet with that faith, Jesus said you can *move mountains*—the mountains of issues the enemy hurls at you.

The bottom line is this:

Unbelief hinders prayers like nothing else. Unbelief agrees with satan.

Counter wise, just as light dispels darkness, belief dispels unbelief. The remedy for unbelief is to build a living belief system from God's living Word. How?

We learned from Scripture that every person on Earth is created in the image of God and gifted with the free will to make choices. What's more, God designed in each of us what I call a "believer device," which simply means you get to decide what you will believe. *What* we believe is formed through our experiences: what we hear, see, and read. And our beliefs affect how we think and what we say. Especially powerful is what we say to ourselves.

Jesus repeatedly emphasized the importance of speaking faith-filled words. When He spoke, he often began with "say" phrases, such as these: "I say to you . . ." and "Whoever says . . . ."

As I shared in an earlier chapter, words are powerful tools—so powerful that they hold life and death. Jesus modeled the "power of the tongue" (Proverbs 18:21) again and again by His spoken words.

Remember the two-sided coin illustration I shared in Chapter 4? The two sides of Heaven's spiritual coin? One side represents *belief* and the other side *faith*—both are required for the coin to have value. To bring Heaven's will to Earth, the spiritual coin's two distinctive sides must work together. Belief and faith are inseparable.

Faith thrives when built on the foundation of unwavering belief.

Consider this Scripture regarding belief:

> Truly Jesus did many other signs in the presence of His disciples, which are not written in this book; but these are written that you may *believe* that Jesus is the Christ, the Son of God, and that *believing* you may have life in His name. — John 20:30–31 (author emphasis)

In the verse, the original Greek word for *believe* is πιστεύω, translated *pisteuó*, a verb that means: "I believe, to have faith, to trust."[26]

In this context, *believe* implies more than just intellectual agreement for what you desire; it conveys your trust in the truth you're agreeing with.

The terms *faith* and *belief* share strikingly similar roots in meaning. While one functions as a noun and the other as a verb, each is essential to the other's fulfillment. Our believer devices alone cannot yield results; we need actions of faith as a result of believing. Likewise, active faith cannot exist without a firm foundation of belief.

Using belief and faith together is the key to receiving from God.

In the following story, you'll see how belief and the smallest mustard seed of faith work together, like a coin, and what that spiritual currency can accomplish.

The Florence Hammill Story

While on furlough from piloting for a major US airline, I had the opportunity to focus on my first jet aviation company, which we operated from our newly built home in Orange County, California. We had transformed our spacious three-car garage into an FAA-approved ground school equipped with visual aids, Cockpit Procedures Trainers, and even three flight simulators. Remarkably, we were the first (and likely the only) FAA-approved classroom in a residential home garage. Paula often teased me for "bringing my work home." We still laugh when we remember those early days.

Paula and I were a team and treated our students like family.

Florence was a pilot in her sixties whom I'd been training weekly for four or five months toward acquiring her instrument rating. We often flew over the Pacific Ocean between Catalina Island and Long Beach as she learned and practiced instrument procedures. As she progressed through the training, we became friends.

An instructor moves at the student's pace early on to ensure they're learning, feeling confident, and enjoying the journey. But when the checkride (practical test) is nearing, my "examiner hat" goes on to confirm the student is prepared to meet every rigorous standard. I took my responsibilities seriously and expected my students to pass. In ten years as an instructor, I'd only had one student checkride failure, and I aimed not to add another.

As Florence and I were closing in on her checkride, she abruptly stopped showing up, and she didn't answer my calls or respond to my messages. The situation was very peculiar.

Soon after her disappearance, I questioned everything about my teaching. *Had I been too tough? Had I offended her? Where had I gone wrong?*

Eventually, I resigned myself to the idea that I'd never know why Florence had quit.

Months later, I received a call from her daughter. She was catching up on her mother's messages and had come across mine. "Dale, did you know my mom had terminal cancer?"

I was stunned. Florence had never mentioned being sick, and I hadn't noticed any signs of illness. Before I could gather a response, she explained. "She didn't want anyone to know." She paused, realizing the news had shocked me. Then she shared, "Flying was Mom's dream. All she wanted was to experience the joy and freedom of flying—and you made that possible."

Ahh . . . , I realized Florence had not intended to get her instrument rating; she simply wanted to enjoy flying as much as possible in her final months. My heart sank deeper. Had I known her flying objectives, I would have focused on making each flight more enjoyable.

"May I visit Florence?"

"Mom's . . . ," she hesitated. "She's in a coma, under hospice care." She paused again and then, as if trying to soften more bad news, tentatively shared, "Visitors aren't allowed. I'm sorry. . . . I'm staying in the room with her."

I was overwhelmed with sadness that I wouldn't have the chance to tell Florence how much I appreciated our time together, nor to try again to share the gospel of Jesus with her as she faced eternity.

God's will was for her to be reborn spiritually, and I felt an urgency to be certain she had the opportunity to choose Heaven as her eternal destination.

After sharing the news with Paula, we prayed together with authority and faith, asking God for three things: that we'd be allowed to see Florence without resistance, that she would be alone so we could pray for her unhindered, and that she'd wake from her coma so we could share the gospel of Jesus with her.

Within the hour, not having spoken with hospice or received permission to see Florence, we headed toward the hospital in faith.

We prayed most of the way, only speaking words of faith and expectation, praising the Lord for hearing and answering our prayers. In the name of Jesus, we rebuked any negative forces vying to interfere. And in faith, we thanked God for allowing Florence to wake from the coma and open her heart to believe the gospel message.

Nothing in the natural realm gave us any hope for success. But in the Spirit—knowing our requests were in agreement with God—we took hold of atomic faith, expecting our prayers to be answered.

Once inside the hospice entrance and standing at the reception desk, I introduced myself as Florence's minister, truthfully so. According to God's Word, every believer in Jesus is a minister of the gospel. Paula and I were acting under the Greek term διάκονοιη found throughout the New Testament (such as 2 Corinthians 6:4), translated *diakonos*, which means "a servant; one who performs any service."[27] Jesus instructed and ordained believers to serve Him by serving others—being His hands, feet, and mouthpiece (Matthew 25:40). Indeed, Paula and I intended to serve Florence as ministers.

The receptionist allowed us through—our first prayer request answered.

The second answer was visible when we entered Florence's room. She was alone.

She barely resembled the vibrant woman we'd known. Her body had wasted away, and her skin was pale and gray.

She was hooked up to an IV and various monitors; the soft beeping seemed in disharmony to my pangs of sorrow at seeing the once-vibrant Florence so frail.

The sound of the machines whisked me years back to my three days in a coma following the airplane crash. I believe that a person in a coma can hear—at least in spirit.

Without hesitation, Paula and I each took one of Florence's hands and began quietly praying aloud, thanking God for her life and asking for His presence in the room.

After a few minutes, Florence's eyelids fluttered and slowly opened. She looked directly at me, our eyes meeting. My heart leaped, and I leaned closer and gently asked, "Florence, can you hear me, sweetheart? Do you know who I am?"

With difficulty, she whispered, "You're . . . my flight . . . instructor . . . Dale."

Chills ran down my arms. God had answered our third prayer. Florence was awake and aware.

Paula and I told her we loved her. We spoke gently, cherishing each moment.

"Florence, do you know if you'll go to Heaven?" I asked.

She looked away, and Paula leaned in. "Florence, do you believe you'll go to Heaven when your life here is over?"

Florence turned back to us, her eyes filled with a deep sadness, and whispered, "It's . . . too late . . . for me."

My heart sank. I knew she believed those words, but I didn't know why. I explained with care, "It's never too late in life, Florence; God's grace is *always* available."

As we sat with our friend, our hands warming hers, we reassured her, "It's not too late. Now is the time to turn to God."

Weak but alert, she looked at me and sighed. Barely audible, she said, "I have nothing . . . to offer Him. . . . I've waited too . . . long."

"You have *everything* to offer," I quickly responded, tenderly squeezing her hand. "You can offer your life to Him right now, and He will give you eternal life with God in Heaven."

"It's . . . too late for me."

Paula shared, "Florence, Jesus told a story in the Bible about the vineyard workers. Some were hired early and worked all day; others came at the last hour. But at the end of the day, the owner paid them all the same wage.

"In this life, some people come to God at the last moment," she explained. "Others follow Him their whole lives. But what matters now is what you choose to do with Jesus—while you can still choose."

Florence whispered regretfully, "I've done nothing . . . for Him, and . . . now there's no time."

I responded, "Jesus came into the world not to judge but to save. Florence, God said to us in His Word that He loves the world so much that He gave His only Son, Jesus, so that whoever believes in Him *will* be saved." I squeezed her now-warm hand and explained the next verse. "God didn't send His Son to condemn us, but to save us—you, me, Paula, and anyone who believes and trusts in Jesus." I paused, watching her process the truth of God's Word and the hope still available to her.

"Florence, if you want to know for *certain* that you'll go to Heaven when this life is done," I urged, "invite Jesus into your heart. Paula and I can help you."

Tears formed in her eyes as she considered the invitation. After a moment, she nodded faintly. "I'd like that," she whispered.

Her fragile voice repeated my words as best she could: "Dear Father, forgive my sins. Thank You for loving and accepting me just as I am. I invite You into my heart and life. I surrender everything to You, Lord Jesus."

Paula smiled and asked her, "Do you know what this means?" Florence shook her head. "It means we're now sisters!"

"And I'm your brother!" I interjected. "When you get to Heaven, you'll be welcomed by *millions* of brothers and sisters." Florence's weary eyes glowed with peace, and a tear of joy slipped down her cheek. "And one day," I promised, "Paula and I will meet you again—in Heaven."

Florence's relief and peace were evident. Her sweet smile set deeper as tears rolled from her eyes. "Thank you," she whispered. Her fragile hands faintly pressed ours. "Thank you . . . for coming here . . . for praying with me."

As we sat with Florence for a few more minutes, delighting in her newfound life, she gently closed her eyes. Her smile softened as she slipped back into a coma. I leaned over and kissed her forehead.

A short while later, we left the room, awestruck by how God had answered our prayers and certain that all of Heaven was rejoicing with us.

"I say to you, there is joy in the presence of the angels of God over one sinner who repents." — Luke 15:10

How grateful we were to see Florence one last time and witness the most significant decision of her life. She had opened her heart to Jesus! Now she had the future of eternal life with Him in Heaven, and we would see her again.

God had answered all our prayers. His will had always been for Florence to accept His gift of salvation. Someone with faith needed to agree with God and be His hands, feet, and mouth to bring His will on Earth as it is in Heaven.

Florence's story reaffirmed a profound truth: God can reach anyone, even in their final moments. We must never tire of sharing His love and the gift of new life in Jesus.

As Paula and I walked silently to our car holding hands, we were filled with awe at God's faithfulness. The joy of a new believer's salvation is almost overwhelming. Florence was now safely in God's hands.

Two weeks later, I received a call from her son. "My mother expressed her wish that her ashes be scattered over the Pacific Ocean, near the Port of Los Angeles, where she'd flown with you."

I felt humbled. Images of our flights flickered through my mind.

"I'll cover any expenses," he hastily added.

"We loved Florence; we'd be honored to do that for her," I replied.

We met at the airport, along with my then-young son, Eric. Florence's son carefully handed me the container bearing his mother's ashes.

Moments later, he watched as our plane rose into the sky for his mother's final earthly flight. The blue expanse of the Pacific stretched beyond and beneath us, shimmering with the sunlight she loved.

After circling a few times, I thanked the Lord again for allowing me to be part of the most important decision Florence ever made. I slowed the airplane and cracked open the passenger door, and we gently released her ashes into the wind. They floated gracefully down and mingled with the ocean waves.

When we landed, Florence's son thanked me with a hug, clearly emotional. Honoring his mother's last wish was his closure—his final goodbye.

He handed me an envelope containing a check and explained, "My mom wanted you to have this. She didn't have much but left this for you."

When I arrived home with the unopened envelope, Paula and I prayed, asking God for guidance where the gift should go. Then we opened the flap, revealing a check for $260—Florence's final gift.

Paula and I looked at each other, remembering her words: "I have nothing to offer Him. I've done nothing for Him, and now there's no time." Yet here she was, giving a heartfelt offering as a seed of faith.

Mark 12 came to my mind. Jesus saw a widow in the temple, giving all her money. The small amount was an enormous offering because it was *all*—everything—she had.

These timeless lessons show the power of a seed, the importance of humility, and the significance of small acts when given with love and trust.

"Paula, we've known for some time that God is calling us to start a nonprofit ministry." His call had been clear to us; we were to preach and teach the gospel of Jesus, sharing all that He had taught us and was still teaching us about faith. The conviction in Paula's expression mirrored mine. "I believe this is what God wants us to do—establish the nonprofit with Florence's donation as its foundation." Paula nodded in wholehearted agreement. Together, we placed our hands on Florence's gift and dedicated it to the Lord. We asked Him to multiply the faith seed for His glory and to Florence's heavenly account.

Florence's gift, the first seed into the ministry, indeed multiplied. Her gift enabled us to eventually reach millions of people in need—body, soul, and spirit—worldwide with the gospel of Jesus and practical supplies. We distributed gospel tracts, Bibles, clothing, food, and medical care, and we produced over eight hundred videos, wrote several books, and accomplished other ministry efforts.

Florence's seed went far.

Eagle International Ministries (aka Dale Black Ministries) grew and thrived for forty-three years, reaching millions of people and bringing tens of thousands to faith in Jesus. Through Florence's seed gift, she was a partner in storing up treasures in heaven, as Matthew 6:20 teaches.

Reflecting on her small seed given in the final hours of her earthly life brings to mind the words of Jesus: "Assuredly, I say to you, if you have faith as small as a mustard seed, you will say to this mountain, 'Move from here to there,' and it will move; nothing will be impossible for you."

God answered Florence's desire to give Him something and supernaturally multiplied her offering *more* than a hundredfold. Florence thought she had nothing to offer. But her gift and faith left an invaluable legacy—a testament to God's power to multiply even the smallest gifts.

Perhaps you're now thinking, "Okay, Capt. Dale, I like your descriptions of faith and how faith works, so I'll give it a try."

No. *Try* dismisses faith. *Try* is not in the faith teachings of Jesus. *Trying* faith is not possible because trying is not faith.

If you say you'll *try* faith, you've already lost.

You must do faith.

Remember, belief and faith are two sides of the same coin; both must work together to receive answers to your prayers. Doubt and belief cannot exist together as darkness cannot exist in light. The enemy will try to tempt you with doubt, but victory comes by holding firm to your beliefs with actions in unwavering faith based on what you truly believe in your heart.

This process requires persistence—repeating your steps of belief and faith over and over until your prayers are answered.

When we ask God for guidance and wisdom, Jesus's teaching through the apostle James applies: "Let him ask in faith, with no doubting, for he who doubts is like a wave of the sea driven and tossed by the wind. For let not that man suppose that he will receive anything from the

Lord; he is a double-minded man, unstable in all his ways" (James 1:6–8).

Receiving answers to prayer doesn't occur with doubt in your heart.

PART FIVE

Power of Faith

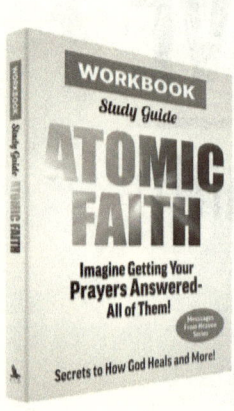

Chapter 17

REAPING THE MIRACULOUS
THE EAGLE SEVEN STORY

To Him who is able to do exceedingly
abundantly above all that we ask or think,
according to the power that works in us.
— Ephesians 3:20

As Jesus performed miracles on Earth, He
repeatedly exposed the secret to answered
prayer: faith in action.

The apostle Paul defined faith for us in Hebrews 11:1:
"Now faith is the substance of things hoped for, the evidence
of things not seen."

By examining this definition, we start to understand
what Jesus demonstrated and taught about how miracles
can be realized through faith.

In my opinion, one of the most important words in this verse is "now." It reveals that faith lives in the present, not the past or future. Faith is *now*. Always right now.

What specific outcome are you praying for?

What do you believe *right now* about that outcome?

This author believes that faith exists in the present moment. Therefore, if you lack faith right now in what you hope for and believe in, the answer to your prayer will be delayed.

Without faith, our beliefs cannot materialize into something we can see and touch.

You can apply the action of faith to anything you hope for and believe in. As an example, let's apply faith to divine healing from God.

If you hope to be healed and you choose to believe that God's promises of healing are available for you, your actions of faith will bring that healing into physical expression.

Your belief in God's promise of healing must be strong in both your heart and your mind.

What Is Faith?

Look again at Hebrews 11:1 and consider the words and phrases I've emphasized in italics.

Now faith is the substance of things *hoped for*.

Once again, we see that hope is the starting point of the faith journey. If you hope for something that God has revealed as His will, such as miraculous healing, and you agree with that outcome, the next step is to turn your hope into firm, unshakable belief in your heart.

Matthew 24:35 tells us that God's Word will never pass away. Everything else we see will pass away, but not His Word. His Word is eternal and true. There is nothing that can defeat the power of God's Word, and only our *belief* and *faith* working together can release that power into our lives.

Jesus *is* the Word. Healing benefits have been paid for and offered to us by Jesus. Now it's up to us to *believe it.*

Once you've rooted your belief in the integrity of God's Word regarding any situation, you'll want to turn your belief into faith. Here's how: Consider the word *substance* in Hebrews 11:1.

Now faith is the *substance* of things hoped for.

When you take action based on what you hope for, believing it's yours, a spiritual substance begins to form in Heaven, similar to how an embryo forms. While the outcome you're hoping and believing for is not yet visible to you, it is a *real* substance seen in the spiritual realm. God sees it. The angels see it. Satan and his demons see it.

The verse continues:

Faith is . . . the *evidence* of things *not seen.*

Your faith is the spiritual *evidence* of what is true and real. Faith is the action you take, based upon what you believe, until . . . the invisible becomes tangible proof.

Your faith is the key that opens Heaven's window, allowing your answer to be revealed in the visible world.

When you express your faith outwardly through actions and words—even though you do not yet see tangible proof—God considers your actions the *evidence* of your faith.

You, others, and certainly God can see your actions demonstrating your conviction in what you're hoping and believing for. That puts you in agreement with God, which allows His will to "be done on earth as it is in Heaven" (Matthew 6:10).

The result: Your actions of faith keep building substance in the spiritual realm until your belief becomes visible. The substance-building and result are somewhat like a pregnancy. You can't see, touch, or feel an embryo in the womb during the early stage. Yet you believe the baby is alive and real—a growing substance. The mother acts daily in faith by speaking about and nourishing the invisible, growing baby she's "expecting."

From the moment you believed, prayed, and acted in faith regarding your circumstance, a faith substance began to form in the unseen realm. Until your request becomes visible, you'll want to stay firm in your faith, expressing your agreement with God's promises through your words and actions. Otherwise, that substance—your faith—will be cut short, and what you're hoping and believing for will not come to pass.

In previous chapters, we explored different ways to express faith—such as persistence, praise, speaking the promises of God, and praying it back. In the following story, you'll discover another action that strengthens your faith powerfully: planting what you already have as a seed.

The Eagle Seven Story

In the mid-1980s, Paula and I took the steps of faith in the life-changing decision I referenced in Florence's story: entering full-time ministry. We surrendered our $12 million business and everything we owned, including lands, homes, and airplanes, to answer that call from God. We believed the path God intended for us was to place our *complete faith* in Jesus and His Word.

Inspired by other ministries using airplanes for humanitarian missions and gospel outreach, I felt led by the Lord to use my background in aviation to contribute to that cause. So, under God's guidance, we founded Eagle International Ministries.

Although we no longer had millions to invest, we had something far more valuable and powerful: *firm belief* and *active faith* that God would provide according to His will and Word.

As you'll recall, our first donation came from Florence, who gave her last $260 after accepting Jesus as her Savior on her deathbed. Her dying wish was to plant a seed toward something good that God could use.

Our vision for the aviation outreach was to acquire a Boeing 707—an airplane I knew well, having flown the 707 as a major airline career pilot and instructor. As I mentioned, several large nonprofit organizations were using large jet aircraft for ministry purposes, and with my background, I was convinced that acquiring that plane was God's will. The purchase would enable our vision: gospel outreach and medical assistance to the poor.

After months of searching, we found a Boeing 707 for sale in Virginia, previously belonging to Eastern Airlines. At $700,000, a four-engine jet with 167 seats seemed reasonable.

Using our limited personal funds, we traveled to Washington, DC, combining a family trip with the business of inspecting the plane. The aircraft was in excellent condition and seemed ideal for humanitarian and gospel outreach.

After some negotiation, the owner and I agreed on a deal worth $650,000, adjusted for inflation. Paula and I were overjoyed, certain that God had provided this opportunity.

That evening, we celebrated in our nation's capital, and I felt at peace, believing the path forward was clear.

A meeting was scheduled for the next morning to finalize the aircraft purchase. I arrived with high expectations, unprepared for a drastic turn of events. The owner was not there, and his secretary handed me the check I'd written the previous day and explained regretfully, "I'm sorry, the plane was sold to someone else."

What? I was stunned. *We had an agreement!*

I had shaken his hand and handed him the check. The disappointment was crushing. I was keenly aware there were no other 707s for sale in the US at the time. The vision we'd been so close to realizing was shattered.

On the flight home, my heart was heavy. I was perplexed as to why God had allowed the purchase to fall through.

I had firmly believed God had given us the answer to our prayers.

Had I misheard God's direction? Where had I gone wrong?

In the following days, I spent long hours alone in the mountains of Julian, California, immersed in prayer and fasting, again seeking God's guidance. A possibility was to take legal action, as our attorney affirmed that we'd entered into a valid agreement with the plane's owner. However, praying over the situation seemed the wisest path, especially in light of past faith experiences. God always faithfully supplied and answered our prayers of faith. I knew He had a better plan, but I wasn't entirely sure of the best course to proceed.

I turned to examples in the Bible and chose to continue praying, fasting, and leaving my concerns in God's hands. I call this process *waiting on God.*

By the fifth day in the mountains, while I read the Bible, prayed, and fasted, God's message grew increasingly clear—clearer than anything I could define. In that sacred moment, Mark 10:29–30 became God's *rhēma* (spoken) word to me.

> Jesus answered and said, "Assuredly, I say to you, there is no one who has left house or brothers or sisters or father or mother or wife or children or lands, for My sake and the gospel's, who shall not receive a hundredfold now in this time—houses and brothers and sisters and mothers and children and lands, with persecutions—and in the age to come, eternal life."

God's still, small voice urged me not to fight for the aircraft or pray for its return. Instead, I sensed Him asking me to let it go and use the situation as a seed-planting of faith, trusting Him for a multiplied blessing. The more I prayed, the clearer the answer became, that God's best was for us to release the aircraft to Him and believe He would resupply us abundantly.

The next day, I informed our attorney that we would not pursue legal action. I then wrote a thoughtful letter to the aircraft's owner thanking him for the opportunity of meeting him and his team and allowing us to view his plane. I acknowledged receiving the check, formally ending the deal, offered him my blessing, and said I would be praying for him.

In the spiritual realm, I had released the plane, and I now stood in faith for a multiplied harvest of God's blessings.

I also wrote to our ministry partners, explaining that we would not pursue legal action. Instead, we would believe God for something better. Certainly, this decision wasn't easy; there were moments of doubt and uncertainty. Yet, to align with God's leading, I took action by speaking His promises over the situation, wholeheartedly believing truth: God is trustworthy and faithful.

The experience taught me valuable lessons that shaped my future and strengthened my confidence in God's still, small voice and *rhĕma* word.

Often what seems like a setback is actually an opportunity to plant a seed for something greater, if we choose to follow God's way. Through this experience, I learned that obedience isn't always about holding on tightly; it's also about trusting God enough to let go when He directs.

Several weeks passed as my faith journey continued for something I could not yet see. No other Boeing 707s were on the market. Persevering in faith during the waiting was essential.

Months passed, and suddenly, another Boeing 707 became available. This plane was in even better condition than the first, with fewer engine hours and a stronger airframe. The downside? A $1.4 million price tag—double our budget.

Once again, I asked God for specific guidance. His response was clear: "Put your faith into action; go see the airplane."

I flew to the aircraft's location, Nashville, and arranged a meeting with the owner, Robert Connors. He was perhaps fifteen years older than me. He was a major landowner and businessman, but he had also built and was managing several regional airlines.

We met at a restaurant, and he began our conversation with a question: "What are you planning to do with the airplane?"

I explained the humanitarian and spiritual work we were already doing—using a smaller aircraft to send teams of volunteers worldwide, providing food and medical care, and, most importantly, sharing the gospel of Jesus Christ.

"Our mission isn't a commercial venture," I added. "It's about serving the needy in practical ways. The airplane will allow us to do more work on a larger scale."

Robert seemed surprised by the goals for the jet and expressed an interest in learning more.

"Robert, what do you know about God?" I inquired. He seemed startled by the question.

After a pause, he shared, "I grew up in church and felt close to God when I was young." He paused again with a distant look in his eyes. "Over the years, work and business have consumed my life." He turned his gaze back to me and said, "Honestly, I haven't thought about God in a long time."

We continued talking, sharing our lives like friends rather than newly-met businessmen. I saw a man weighed down by the pressures of life.

I shared about the airplane crash that almost killed me and how it changed me. Tears welled in his eyes, and he spoke about his personal struggles and business. Beneath all the talk of airplanes and corporate deals, I sensed a deeper need. His soul seemed tired.

Abruptly, as if to move past his feelings, Robert asked, "Do you want to go see the airplane?" But God's Spirit was pounding on my heart.

"Robert, from God's perspective, you are far more important than any airplane. You're more important to God than anything else happening."

He looked surprised, and again, his eyes filled with tears. He lowered his head and spoke about his mistakes, his empty life, and how far he had drifted from God.

We were both emotional—an odd sight; two businessmen in suits, in tears, at a restaurant table. "Robert, what do you think would happen if you got right with God again? What would change in your life? In your business and family?" His face contorted. "What's holding you back from asking God to forgive you and inviting Jesus to take full control of your life?"

Earnest compassion pulled me from our surroundings, and I reached out my hand and asked, "Robert, would you like to pray together?" He looked away and briefly hesitated. Then he nodded and placed his hand in mine. In that moment, he made a heart- and life-altering decision. He took a step of faith toward God, healing, and peace. We bowed our heads, and I led him in a prayer of recommitment to Jesus.

I lifted my head and saw transformation on Robert's face. The weariness seemed to have lifted, replaced by a lightness and less stress. He started chuckling, which I sensed was part of his releasing pent-up pressure, having spent years running from God. Then he paused and grew serious. "Thank you, Dale. Thank you very much."

"Oh, sir, no, not me. Thank the Lord! He loves you so very much, and it's always a privilege to help anyone reconnect with Jesus."

After a moment, Robert smiled big and said, "Well, Dale, do you want to go see the airplane now?" We both grinned; this was the third time he'd asked, and I felt released to say yes. God's primary business had been completed.

Parked outside the hangar was a beautiful Boeing 707. After a full exterior walk around, it was clear that this 707 was in far better condition than the one I'd lost in Virginia.

"So, what do you think?" Robert asked.

I was honest. "You're asking $1.4 million, and it's worth every penny. But I don't have that kind of money. My wife and I gave up everything to follow God's call. The most I can offer is a fraction of that."

"Well, Dale, how much can you offer?"

I reached into my pocket and pulled out a check for $650,000, filled out but unsigned. I handed it to Robert. He looked at the figure and turned his head, looking into the distance, silent.

The moment was incredibly awkward for me. I had seen far too many ministers, pastors, and missionaries manipulate and pressure hard-working businessmen and women for money "in the name of the Lord." The coercing had left a bad taste in my mouth for decades. At the same time, my duty was to follow God and do as He directed.

Robert then turned back to me with a smile. "I'll do it! The plane is yours."

I couldn't believe it. I'd later realize my initial response was odd, given that I had stood firm in faith for God to fulfill His Mark 10 multiplication promise, yet my first reaction was surprise and disbelief.

His promise of a multiplied return was unfolding right before my eyes. I had released the first airplane in faith, believing God had something greater in store, and here it was! An even better commercial jet at a price we could afford. On top of that was a greater joy: having been part of Robert's spiritual renewal and transformation in following Jesus.

But Robert wasn't finished.

"Dale, I need to confess something." He smiled sheepishly and nodded toward the plane. "The nose gear has a small crack in it. I can't give something to God with a flaw like that. I'll replace it before you take delivery."

Again, I was stunned, speechless. My head was doing the math: A new nose gear and the labor would easily cost around $100,000. Robert knew the cost.

"Don't worry," he insisted, reading my thoughts. "I'll cover it." Relief and wonder washed over me. "Do you have money for fuel?"

I shook my head. "No, sir. I don't."

"Dale, do you know how much it'll cost to fly this plane from here to California?" I hadn't thought that far ahead because I hadn't planned on buying this airplane. God had only told me to go see it.

Before I could answer, Robert did. "It'll be over $109,000—in fuel alone." He was still smiling and laid a hand on my shoulder. "Don't worry; I'll cover that cost too."

I was still speechless. Amazement and awe flowed through me at what God was doing in abundance. His extravagant work through Robert, a man who had just returned to Him, was overwhelming. Robert was willing to be used by God as a vessel of blessing in this pivotal situation, just as Florence had. Giving to God is not about quantity but about the heart.

Then, as if in afterthought, Robert asked, "Do you have life jackets?" Puzzled, I asked him to clarify.

He explained, "Our sales literature for the 707 says it doesn't come with life preservers. And you can't legally take off in a plane without life jackets, even if you don't have passengers."

I hadn't considered that. The plane seated 167 people. I'd had no idea we would need that many life jackets.

Before I could recover my voice, Robert said, "Don't worry about it; I'll take care of that too. When you come to get the airplane, it'll have a life jacket for every seat."

I felt humbled and uncomfortable, not knowing how to accept such generosity—from anyone. The extraordinary blessings of Heaven that had just unfolded before me, one after another, left me numb with awe.

I replayed the gifts in my thoughts: Robert had agreed to sell the aircraft at fifty cents to the dollar and offered to repair the nose gear, cover the astonishing fuel cost, *and* provide the life jackets, all at no additional cost to our organization. And I hadn't even seen the inside of the aircraft yet!

"Do you have pilots to fly the plane?" Robert asked.

I smiled, feeling that I could at least offer something. "Yes, sir. Don't worry about that. I've got pilots—and I'll be the captain."

Robert grinned. "Okay, let's see the inside."

Inspecting the interior, I found it was also more than I'd hoped for. The 707 was in pristine condition! I couldn't have been more elated and amazed. Truly, God had multiplied His blessing beyond my ability to conceive.

We paid the same amount for this airplane that we would have for the one in Virginia. But we received a far superior aircraft and exceedingly more. Best of all, I acquired a new spiritual brother for eternity.

What stood out most was how God prioritizes the spiritual over the physical. Long before I'd laid eyes on this second airplane, God had been working in Robert's heart. Through my prayers, fasting, and unwavering faith in God's perfect timing, He orchestrated the circumstances that brought Robert and me together for that miraculous encounter.

Our petition for an airplane was a deal made in the heavenly realm first. It gained substance by our faith in action, patience, and trust in God's Word and His faithfulness. Then the plane became visible and real in the natural—more abundantly than I could have imagined. God's kingdom principles had played out. What was seemingly lost (the first aircraft) was greatly multiplied back to us.

Through obedience, atomic faith, and confidence in God's leading, He gave us far more than we had expected. Plus He had begun a new work in Robert, his family, and his business.

As I reflected on that phenomenal experience, I was reminded of the truth of Ephesians 3:20: "Now to Him who is able to do exceedingly abundantly above all that we ask or think, according to the power that works in us."

Isn't that Scripture to our natural response interesting? We don't seem to struggle with the knowledge that God *can* do exceedingly abundantly above all that we ask or think. We often overlook that He *does* provide according to His power that *works in us*: our hope, belief, and atomic faith.

We are truly in a partnership with God to bring His will to Earth.

God does exceedingly abundantly more than we expect—according to the power that works in us.

When we took possession of the Boeing 707, everything was perfectly prepared: The plane was fully fueled, the nose gear repaired, and the life jackets securely in place. The timing was incredibly wonderful. I took off, flying the 167-passenger jet back to California on July 18, the anniversary of the airplane crash I had miraculously survived.

The blessings were profound testaments to God's power working through hope, belief, and faith. Yet another experience that serves as a powerful reminder of what I call *atomic faith*.

God's ways always surpass our ways.

Looking back, I see now that letting go of the first airplane wasn't a loss; it was an act of obedience and trust in God that opened the door to something far greater. What seemed like a sacrifice was actually a seed planted in faith, bringing a multiplied return.

God's ways always exceed our own. Without faith, what we believe remains unseen. With faith, the impossible becomes possible.

Chapter 18

FAITH UNDER FIRE
THE ROBERT MACINTIRE STORY

Count it all joy when you fall into various
trials, knowing that the testing of your
faith produces patience. But let patience
have its perfect work, that you may be
perfect and complete, lacking nothing.
— James 1:2–4

FAITH CAN BE EXPRESSED IN MANY WAYS, VARYING BY OUR CHALLENGES. Receiving answered prayer regarding a difficult circumstance requires taking a stand of faith and exercising the *traits of faith*. One trait of effective faith is almost always required: *persistence*.

A description of persistence is *perseverance,*[28] which requires endurance and patience. At least one of those attributes is always part of any successful faith journey. For example, the desire for healing often requires all four.

We persevere for whatever time is necessary for faith to fulfill its work: the visible answer to a prayer.

Sadly, many people prematurely let go of their faith during a challenge due to the negative and discouraging circumstances, reports, and opinions of others.

A common tactic of satan is to use what we can see, hear, touch, smell, or feel—the visible—which often robs people of their faith—the invisible.

But for the enemy to win our challenges, we must agree with him rather than God. We always have two choices: remain in faith, agreeing with God's Word against negative tactics, or let go of faith, agreeing with the enemy.

Let's do a brief exercise:

1. Think back to a difficult time when your prayers were not answered.
2. What prompted you to quit believing?
3. At what point and why did you let go of what you hoped or believed for?

An important part of practicing atomic faith is to reevaluate what happened in your past that caused you to let go of your faith. This practice will help you become better prepared to circumvent the enemy with greater persistence, perseverance, endurance, and patience in faith.

I'm grateful to the Lord Jesus for my many faith battles. Each challenge allowed me the opportunity to practice and grow stronger in each various aspect of atomic faith, enabling me to endure to the end, winning the victories.

The occasional very lengthy battles were unusually challenging to overcome. Many people said to me, "That's impossible! You'll never . . . ," etc.

The most difficult challenges pushed me to apply and practice the traits of faith with persistence to endure. Practice strengthened my belief in God's Word and His faithfulness, preparing me for bigger battles ahead.

God graciously warned us to expect resistance. 1 Peter 4:12 (AMP) tells us this:

> Beloved, do not be surprised at the fiery ordeal which is taking place to test you [that is, to test the quality of your faith], as though something strange or unusual were happening to you.

Satan comes to steal the Word of God from our hearts, and God allows our faith to be tested to reveal its purity and strength. Knowing that challenges to our faith accomplish great victories on our behalf, we need to embrace the testing and choose to endure with perseverance.

The testing of our faith helps us grow stronger.

I think of young David's story in 1 Samuel 17:34–36. While courageously volunteering to go up against Goliath the giant, he recounted to King Saul how God had previously used a lion and a bear to teach him that with God's help, he could be victorious. He had withstood those previous tests and grown in his faith, which qualified him to win the Goliath victory—a battle with far greater risk against a more difficult enemy.

Learning the principles of faith and practicing faith's traits—*perseverance* with persistence, endurance, and patience—in every small challenge will prepare you to overcome the bigger challenges ahead.

In considering how to illustrate the power of persistence in faith, no other person looms greater in my mind than Dr. Robert MacIntire. What a powerful testimony he built with his persistent faith. Enjoy this story.

The Robert MacIntire Story

Dr. Robert MacIntire and I first met when he enrolled in my company's Jet Type Rating Course for training on the Cessna Citation. I had the privilege of becoming not only Dr. Bob's flight instructor and examiner but also a personal friend.

As I reflected on my career, having trained over a thousand professional pilots, Bob stood out as one of the most likable, driven, and teachable.

A devout Catholic, Dr. Bob deeply respected his religion and even raised a son who became a priest. Yet Bob had never encountered a personal relationship with God through Jesus Christ.

Bob admitted he lacked understanding of his need for a Savior. He was unaware of God's requirement that we each personally accept Jesus's sacrifice on the cross for our sins. Only through the righteousness of Jesus could Bob (and you and I) enter a relationship with a holy God.

I shared with Bob 1 Timothy 2:5, "There is one God and one Mediator between God and men [mankind], the Man Christ Jesus." And I explained that no priest, not even the pope, could intercede between him and God. Only Jesus, God's Son, could intercede. As Jesus said in John

14:6, "I am the way, the truth, and the life. No one comes to the Father except through Me."

One evening after flight training, Bob and I talked extensively about what the Bible teaches regarding our need for a Savior. I showed him in the Bible that eternal life in Heaven with Jesus is available to those who believe in Him: "As many as received Him, to them He gave the right to become children of God, to those who believe in His name" (John 1:12).

"Bob, no personal effort or sacrifice can earn God's favor," I continued. "He requires us to acknowledge our sin. It's sin that separates people from a holy God. We must each repent to Him and ask Him to forgive us and save us. By accepting Jesus's sacrifice on the cross in our place, we can invite Him into our hearts and lives."

I flipped the Bible pages to Romans 5:8 and read it aloud: "God demonstrates His own love toward us, in that while we were still sinners, Christ died for us." Then I flipped to Acts 6:31 and read that we must "believe on the Lord Jesus Christ" as our personal Savior to be saved.

Later that evening, the Lord graciously used me to guide Bob into the family of God. What an incredible privilege!

That same evening, Bob also asked God to fill him with His Holy Spirit! Bob's transformation was unmistakable. His actions proved he was serious about his repentance and asking Jesus to lead his life. His zest for life and learning were reflections of his faith in Jesus. His new birth in Christ supercharged him.

After Dr. Bob began his spiritual journey with little knowledge of God or His Word, he quickly became a strong man of faith. I had given him a Bible, and he wasted no time devouring it as if his life depended on it. I was thrilled and thankful to see him taking every *logos* Word of God to heart, believing firmly in everything God's Word said, regardless of overwhelming circumstances to the contrary.

Before his spiritual birth, Bob's marriage was in ruins. His wife had filed for divorce and wanted nothing more to do with him. However, after he'd committed his life to Jesus and received the Holy Spirit, he prayed for God to remake him from the inside out. With unwavering faith, Bob believed God's Word and persistently believed God for the restoration of his marriage.

On the divorce court date, he stood before the judge with his wife and some of their children. When the judge asked Bob why he was seeking reconciliation, Bob boldly declared, "Because I am a brand-new man. Jesus lives inside of me, and I'm full of love for my wife and children. Your Honor, I love her and will care for her with every fiber of my being."

He then placed his Bible on the courtroom floor, and in that decisive moment, he stood on it and declared, "I'm standing on the Word of God for the restoration of my marriage. I have faith that God will answer my prayer. Please, Your Honor, do not sign those divorce papers."

Despite his heartfelt plea, the judge granted the divorce.

> What would you have done in that circumstance? It seemed that Bob's faith had not worked. He had put it all on the line, so where was God?

> Would you have accepted the belief that God wouldn't answer your prayer for a restored marriage? Would you have given up?
>
> What do you think went wrong?

Over the next year, Bob lost more than his marriage. He lost his lucrative dental and oral surgery practice, his large ranch in the Northwest, and his beloved airplane. Completely broke, he spent many nights living in his car and always studying the Bible.

Bob was part of our daily lives, in person and by phone. Paula and I regularly answered his questions, taught him how faith works, and stressed this truth:

God's Word does not fail.

As Bob consistently and persistently read and studied the Bible, he grew stronger in his belief in God and His Word and continued fighting his battles with the power of faith.

Despite the overwhelming negative circumstances, Bob remained unfazed and persisted daily in calling out to God with atomic faith: "Thank you, Father, for making me a new man. Thank you for restoring my marriage and giving me another chance. Thank You, dear Jesus, for giving me new life."

> Consider again Matthew 6:33: "Seek first the kingdom of God and His righteousness, and all these things shall be added to you."

The Holy Spirit led Bob to do what was needed: He spent time in prayer and the Bible and held firmly to faith for what he desired—his marriage restored.

Through all the difficulty, Bob could have chosen to give up. There were many times when his prayers seemed hopelessly futile. After all, the man had lost everything. And while he relentlessly made every attempt to be a father to his children, his unbelieving wife consistently resisted his proclamation of faith that God would restore their marriage.

Under the dire circumstances, did Bob let go of his faith? Did he give up on believing God would answer his prayers? I can honestly say that in every conversation I had with him, he did not! He persisted in faith daily, month after month, never letting go of God's Word or His promise to return what the enemy had stolen (2 Corinthians 9:10–15).

Bob's words and actions consistently reflected his atomic faith in God's faithfulness and that his marriage would be restored.

Benefits of Persistence

Dr. Bob's approach often reminded me of a parable in which Jesus said,

"Men always ought to pray and not lose heart. . . . There was in a certain city a judge who did not fear God nor regard man. Now there was a widow in that city; and she came to him, saying, 'Get justice for me from my adversary.' And he would not for a while; but afterward he said within himself, 'Though I do not fear God nor regard man, yet because this widow troubles me I will avenge her, lest by her continual coming she weary me.'"

Then the Lord said, "Hear what the unjust judge said. And shall God not avenge His own elect who cry out day and night to Him, though He bears long with them? I tell you that He will avenge them speedily. Nevertheless, when the Son of Man comes, will He really find faith on the earth?" — Luke 18:1–8

Bob convinced his ex-wife, Jill, to visit our home with him. Later she told us, "I assumed you were crazy fanatics, but I wanted to see for myself." To her surprise, we enjoyed a pleasant and friendly dinner as we shared the love of Jesus with her. Shortly after, Jill invited Jesus into her heart.

A few days later, she was filled with the Holy Spirit. And within ten days, she and Bob remarried—this time rooted in the Lord and His Word.

The change in their hearts and marriage was as if a dam of blessings had broken open and suddenly flooded their lives.

Dr. Bob's atomic faith had visibly manifested the answers to his prayers. The outcome was a testament to God's faithfulness.

1. Bob first regained *hope* when he was spiritually reborn and learned that God's will was to restore his marriage.
2. Bob began to build *belief* in his heart as he read God's Word and *believed* it was true.
3. Bob then built his *faith* through words and actions.
4. Bob persistently *acted* according to what he *believed*, regardless of the contrary circumstances.

Dr. Bob and Jill pursued their new spiritual life and grew strong in faith. Throughout the next couple of years, Bob became a gifted leader and minister in the body of Christ. He and Jill continually shared their testimony wherever possible.

Eventually, they launched a daily Christian television program, sharing the transformative power of God's love and helping tens of thousands of couples and families.

God's mighty work through Bob and Jill included ministering to actors Gavin and Patti MacLeod. Bob played a crucial role in guiding the couple to trust God as they pursued restoring their broken marriage.

Bob's and Jill's lives have left an eternal impact on many, standing as a testament to God's transformative power through hope, belief, and faith.

After a full life into his nineties, Dr. Bob entered Heaven.

What a privilege for me to share with you the last email I received from him:

> *From the moment you taught me to fly jet aircraft, Capt. Dale, and realized I wasn't a born-again Christian, you began leading me to the Lord. You accomplished*

what no one else had done for me, and words can never express my gratitude.

Thank you, Dale & Paula, for leading me to the Lord, for caring for me, and always sharing God's love. I'll always be grateful to be your co-pilot.

Bob's drive and commitment were reflected through his many gifts and accomplishments. He earned film awards showcasing innovative dental maxillofacial procedures, held five oral and maxillofacial device patents, developed three groundbreaking dental procedures that revolutionized oral surgery, and had two major university biomechanical labs named in his honor.

Dr. Bob served for over twenty years as the primary physician on numerous evangelistic mission trips Paula and I led through our Eagle International Ministries organization. He performed surgeries, cared for the poor, taught God's Word, and regularly shared his testimony. Remarkably, he always offered his time and medical expertise free of charge.

Though Bob's earthly gain had earlier crumbled, God restored not only his marriage but eventually his wealth, similar to what God did for Job in the Old Testament.

Exercising faith with persistence, perseverance, endurance, and patience, Bob once again became a multimillionaire—but this time fully surrendered to the One who'd saved him and restored his marriage: the Lord Jesus.

Bob and Jill lived out Matthew 6:33. Bob said repeatedly, "I'm seeking first the Kingdom of God and His righteousness. Whatever money God brings me through patents and my efforts, well, that's His business."

Beyond our ministry work together, Bob and I had grown close as friends. Our families even shared several vacations over the years. He was my dear personal friend and a brother in Christ to all who belonged to God's family.

Bob was survived by his loving wife—our dear friend Jill—his children, and many grandchildren and great-grandchildren.

One life *can* change the world when that person is committed to Jesus and is using atomic faith to bring Heaven's will to Earth. Bob took God's Word literally and believed:

With God nothing is impossible!

Followers of Jesus are offered the victory of overcoming in all things. But victory costs something.

Too often, I find that followers of Jesus today believe that miracles no longer happen and that we don't have access to the power of God. But we do! Throughout this book we've seen examples of true current-day miracles, each traced back to *persistent faith*.

With persistence, hold tightly to hope, belief, and faith throughout your battles.

Although Bob's prayers had seemed impossible and the answer had taken months to materialize visibly, he received victory through his anchored belief in God's Word and actions taken with atomic faith.

How?

- Full trust in God
- Belief in the Word of God
- Persistent actions of faith in agreement with what he believed

The impossible can become possible for those who do things God's way.

> Let us hold fast the confession of our hope without wavering, for He who promised is faithful.
> — Hebrews 10:23

Faith Is Required From Beginning to End

Faith is the conduit for spiritual birth and growth. We need faith to become born-again in Jesus. And we need faith for every step of our journey forward.

As you read the verse below, notice the underlined words, each a *faith action* based on what a person believes in their heart.

> If you <u>confess</u> with your mouth the Lord Jesus and <u>believe</u> in your heart that God has raised Him from the dead, you will be saved. For with the heart one <u>believes</u> unto righteousness, and with

the mouth <u>confession</u> is made unto salvation. — Romans 10:9–10 (author emphasis)

A foremost reason I wrote this book was to reignite a longing in people's hearts for the abundant life God instills in us through His Spirit when we receive Jesus as our Savior. Thereby, I urge you to place Jesus at the center of your heart and life.

Make Jesus your everything!

Chapter 19

SUPERCHARGE YOUR PRAYERS
THE RUSSIAN DISCO REVIVAL STORY

To Him who is able to do exceedingly
abundantly above all that we ask or think,
according to the power that works within us.
— Ephesians 3:20

EVERY FOLLOWER OF JESUS HAS BEEN GIVEN POWERFUL TOOLS FROM GOD'S KINGDOM TO USE ON EARTH. Faith is what gives us the ability to use those tools effectively. God designed these spiritual power tools to bring His will into our daily lives—on Earth as it is in Heaven. One of the most important tools is communication.

The Benefits of Communication

Consider how a military leader requires clear communication with their troops to convey the enemy's location, instruct appropriate weapons, outline the most effective strategy for navigating and winning the battle, and take action.

Likewise, God is our spiritual Commander. He desires to direct every aspect of our lives for our safety and the "exceedingly abundantly" best outcome described in the key verse above.

We know from previous chapters that He's given us His *logos* orders in the Bible and His *rhēma* wisdom and instruction through His Spirit. But unfortunately, we won't hear His *rhēma* word or discern His *logos* direction unless our spiritual frequency is tuned to His divine channel: the Holy Spirit within you.

As followers of Jesus, we can learn to hear our Commander clearly by reading and studying the Bible and listening for His communications within our spirits.

Sadly, our flesh nature is often more dominant than our spirit, and in those times, we cannot receive or clearly hear or understand His communication. Our lack of connection to our Commander within us leaves us vulnerable in life's battles.

How do you change that?

Strengthen your spirit through prayer and fasting.

Fasting is one of the most intriguing, meaningful, and powerful practices Jesus taught His followers for effectively hearing God and communicating with Him.

Supercharge Your Prayers by Fasting

Fasting means abstaining from food or certain comforts for a set period. However, Jesus taught that fasting goes beyond skipping a meal or a comfort. Fasting accompanies prayer as a *supercharger*.

Fasting is a spiritual tool meant to

- sensitize your spirit,
- suppress your flesh, and
- focus your prayers and spiritual ears in
- preparation for important moments of directions and decisions.

I'm convinced that the experience I share below would not have occurred had I not first fasted. My spirit heard God's instructions clearly in crucial and unexpected moments that radically changed hundreds of lives—mine included.

The Russian Disco Revival Story

As the Berlin Wall fell and the winds of change swept through Eastern Europe, I led a team of eighteen on a mission trip to Russia. The group consisted of laypeople who loved the Lord, knew how to pray, and had a heart for those who didn't personally know Jesus.

Before our departure, I emphasized the importance of praying and fasting. "This practice is central to our effectiveness," I explained. "The purpose of fasting with prayer is to deepen our spiritual focus, increase our sensitivity to the Holy Spirit's voice and leading, and unify our team."

The team agreed to fast and pray before we traveled to Moscow.

On our third evening in Russia, we prepared for an evening at Moscow's famed outdoor amusement park, Gorky Park. Our guide for that outing was a dignified professor from Moscow State University. Anatoly was about fifty, tall, impeccably dressed, and a product of the Soviet culture and education system. He was openly atheist, the norm in Soviet Russia. Anyone affiliated with the state was mandated to renounce religious beliefs to work in public roles.

Anatoly had brought his mother along—a shy older woman who couldn't speak a word of English. Reserved and reluctant to even shake our hands, she followed along quietly as we explored the park.

Gorky Park wasn't quite what I had expected. The description had conjured thoughts of Russia's answer to Disneyland. The disappointment was that the park lacked the grandeur and thrill of American theme parks. The few simple rides and old-fashioned attractions sat in a modest environment. However, as we strolled farther, we encountered a massive pavilion blaring disco music.

Hundreds of people were packed on what had become a dance floor. Clearly, we had stumbled upon the park's main attraction, a hub. Brightly dressed young people, reminiscent of *Saturday Night Fever*, danced energetically to Western rock and Russian pop hits.

The dim lighting and chilly air seemed suddenly brighter and warmer by the unrestrained expression of freedom—perhaps a direct response to the newfound openness of their country. Communism had fallen. The excitement bursting from the structure was palpable.

By the time we met with the surprise, Anatoly's reserved demeanor had softened with curiosity about our group and what had brought us to Russia. Several team members shared stories with him during our stroll, speaking openly about their relationship with Jesus and experiences back home.

Though Anatoly remained respectfully silent on matters of faith, his open-mindedness to listen surprised me. By the end of the evening, he would become more than a guide; Anatoly would become a dear friend.

With physical and spiritual eyes, I saw a nation transitioning after years of isolation, eager for connection and understanding. As I observed the joyous crowd molded into the pavilion, an inner prompting struck me. I was to somehow interact with the energetic group, so I acted on that inner sensing. "Anatoly, would you be willing to talk with the event organizers and ask permission for me to speak to the crowd—as an airline pilot from America," I explained, "and the only survivor of a plane crash?"

Anatoly obliged, and a few minutes later, he returned with permission granted. "You have three minutes," he instructed, "after the next song, which will last four minutes."

A surge of energy ignited me. I quickly gathered the team, and we prayed for God's guidance.

Moments later, the music stopped, and I humbly took the platform facing over six hundred curious faces. I trusted God to give our group favor. Standing supportively behind me was my team of eighteen.

The DJ signaled me to start, and I took the mic and introduced myself as an airline pilot from the United States. Anatoly graciously translated word for word, and I shared our group's reason for being there. "We're here to tell you something important: Jesus Christ is the Messiah." I briefly paused and Anatoly translated.

"Jesus is alive," I boldly shared, "and His Spirit desires to live in you! Each of you—every person." Again, Anatoly's voice resounded in Russian with the customary enthusiasm of an interpreter.

I recounted being the only survivor of an airplane crash and how the experience had transformed me from the inside out. I spoke of realizing my identity as a person created and loved by God. Line by line, Anatoly respectfully repeated every word.

"Jesus has saved me and given me new life!"

"Lisus spas menya I dal mne novuyu zhizn'," Anatoly echoed.

I glanced at the DJ, expecting my time was up, but he surprised me with a smile and gestured to continue. With newfound freedom, I spoke of how the Cold War had once made enemies of our nations, "Yet with God, we can be brothers and sisters."

"Odnako s Bogom my mozhem byt' brat'yami i sestrami."

"God's love is universal, uniting us all—Americans, Russians, Europeans. Even the French!" That earned a few laughs.

I felt Anatoly drawing nearer to my side as he translated. Despite his atheism, he faithfully conveyed my testimony, telling the crowd about my relationship with Jesus.

"When I came out of a three-day coma, I had a new perspective on life," I explained. "Though I was still imperfect as a human being, God had profoundly changed me inside."

I instinctively patted my heart, and Anatoly did the same as he repeated in Russian, "Bog gluboko izmenil menya iznutri."

"Now, more than anything, I want others to know the joy and meaning that Jesus has given me." I introduced my team, emphasizing that we had each found peace and purpose through faith in Jesus. "If you want to find true meaning and purpose in your life, you'll find it only in Jesus Christ."

Through Anatoly's fluent and expressive Russian, the message reached hundreds of hearts in a way I hadn't anticipated.

As he was speaking, something unexpected caught my eye. His mother, standing off to the side just below the platform, was weeping. Tears ran down her face, but clearly she was rejoicing in hearing her atheist son sharing the good news of Jesus. Questions erupted in me. *Perhaps she's one of the countless Christians who survived the strictly mandated atheism by remaining silent about her faith. For how long? Forty years?*

The tidal wave of thoughts seemed to pause time. *Could she have been praying all these years for her son's salvation? And now she's witnessing him preaching the gospel of Jesus?*

Something powerful was happening. Anatoly may not have believed the gospel message he was delivering, but he was hearing it—possibly for the first time. His mother, so moved, seemed to loom tall as a testament to her endurance of faith despite decades of suppression.

I asked the attentive crowd, "How many of you want to know, beyond a doubt, that when your life ends, you'll go to Heaven? To know with certainty," I explained, "believe that Jesus is the Son of God. Ask Him to forgive your sins and invite Him into your heart, and live your life for Him."

Immediately, I was inspired to share something unusual. "I just came from the Kremlin, where I saw beautiful murals and paintings depicting the life of Jesus—His birth, His death, and His resurrection." I paused briefly to let that fact settle into their hearts.

"Even in your Kremlin, the Holy Spirit is shown descending from Heaven and filling the disciples with His power." I searched the hundreds of eyes, witnessing a realization across the sea of faces. "Your capital . . . ," I paused, "proclaims the *same message* we're sharing with you tonight." I had gestured toward Anatoly and now turned to the team behind me. Indicating them with my outstretched arm, I told the crowd, "None of us are perfect, but we've each repented of our sins and accepted the free gift Jesus offers: salvation."

I turned back to the mass. "We're forgiven! Jesus is alive in us. And we know we'll be with God someday." I pointed to the heavens. "That confidence is something each of you can have too."

Anatoly interpreted every word. ". . . kazhdyy iz vas tozhe mozhet imet."

"If you'd like to receive Jesus into your heart and life now, let me lead you in prayer. I'm going to count to three, and if you're ready to receive Jesus as your Savior, move forward, come up near the front, and I'll pray with you."

In preparation for such an opportunity, I had practiced counting to three in Russian. I looked at Anatoly and carefully counted into the microphone, "Odin, dva, tri."

As soon as "tri" left my lips, the entire mass moved toward us, closing the gaps. The overwhelming response was so unexpected, I thought something in translation had gone wrong. *Did they misunderstand my attempt at Russian—or the invitation I offered?*

I glanced at Anatoly, whose bewilderment mirrored mine. I whispered, "Did I say something wrong? Did you translate it correctly?" I wasn't accusatory but concerned that something was amiss; almost everyone had moved toward me, their expectant faces locked on mine.

He leaned in, "I said exactly what you said—and we counted correctly."

Relieved, though still taken aback, I caught sight of his mother. Her beaming face and sparkling tears encouraged me, and I repeated the message to ensure the crowd understood. "Jesus Christ died for you and me. He shed His blood to pay for our sin."

Anatoly repeated, "On prolil Svoyu krov', chtoby zaplatit' za nashi grehi."

"The message I'm sharing is displayed in your Kremlin." I gestured northward. "The message of salvation—of new life.

"One day, all of us will leave this Earth. But if you choose Jesus, you can know now—right now—that you'll go to Heaven when that day comes." I paused and Anatoly interpreted.

"If you'd like to receive Jesus, we have a gospel tract and a Russian-translated Bible for you."

Briefly, I looked behind me and signaled the team to each raise a hand. I said again to the crowd, "On the count of three, raise your hand if you want to receive Jesus." I raised my hand and held it high, and Anatoly did the same and translated. I counted in English, demonstrating with my fingers, "One, two, three."

"Odin, dva, tri," Anatoly repeated.

As he landed on "tri," hands shot up throughout the crowd, and I knew they had understood the invitation. Faces showed genuine eagerness to know Jesus. Perhaps many had only heard about Him in whispers from grandparents or other aged relatives. For some, the gospel truth I'd delivered may have been their first to hear of Jesus.

That night in Moscow, as we witnessed faith spring from those who believed the salvation message, we also saw in them an overwhelming hope, a yearning to know more about the love and forgiveness Jesus offers.

The magnetic response to the Holy Spirit was a striking reminder that the message of Jesus resonates universally. Regardless of language, culture, or belief differences, the living Word reaches those who hunger for truth and peace.

As the team stepped forward, I invited the crowd to repeat a prayer I would lead them through. With our hands extended, I led the simple prayer, each line translated by Anatoly:

"Dear God, I believe in Jesus as the Messiah, the Son of God. I believe He died for my sins. Please forgive me and come into my life. In Jesus's name, amen."

There were tears, smiles, hugs, and even some jumping among the hive of new believers. And there were the team's outbursts of praise to God.

As we wrapped up, the DJ still appeared unfazed by our interruption to the festivities. He resumed the music, and the dancing came alive again, this time with a new pulse— the heart of God.

We remained nearby, answering questions, praying for people, and listening to their stories. Many spoke broken English, and we lacked Russian, but that didn't stop the flow of conversation and connection.

Our team had arrived in Russia prepared for whatever God had in store, carrying nine hundred Russian-translated Bibles and gospel tracts. By the time we'd finished ministering to individuals, couples, and small groups over the next two hours, every tract and Bible had been dispersed. Eventually, that night, hundreds of people would carry the Word of God through the city and into their homes—and hopefully into their hearts and lives.

> So many people are waiting around the world for the gospel. Even here in the US, more people than ever have not yet heard the priceless message.

Who will tell them?

> How then shall they call on Him in whom they have not believed? And how shall they believe in Him of whom they have not heard? And how shall they hear without a preacher? And how shall they preach unless they are sent?
> — Romans 10:14–15

Stepping out into uncomfortable or unfamiliar situations requires *faith*, but prayer paves the way and opens doors and hearts.

Romans 10:15 continues with a description of Heaven's view of those who fulfill Jesus's commission to spread the gospel: "How beautiful are the feet of those who preach the gospel of peace, who bring glad tidings of good things!"

One of the most touching moments was a conversation with Anatoly's mother. She was over the moon, still in tears of joy, and shared through an interpreter that she had been in hiding for decades as a Christian, praying for her son all those years. "I dreamed of seeing this," she whispered. "Tonight, I heard my son speak of Jesus!"

Our team boarded our bus, tired yet grateful for the enormous spiritual harvest. As we moved toward our hotel, a team member approached me, expressing concern for Anatoly. "Something's wrong," she said.

Anatoly sat quietly in the front seat, his mother just behind him. I moved forward, sat beside him, and asked, "Are you feeling all right, Anatoly?" He nodded, his gaze fixed downward. "Are you thinking about what happened tonight?" His face was marked with emotion.

"Yes," he whispered.

"I've met many people over the years, but few as intelligent and distinguished as you, Anatoly. Yet we must each humble ourselves to connect with God," I explained, "and we can only do that through Jesus."

He listened intently.

I caught a glimpse of his mother, and our eyes met. She knew she was witnessing the answer to her years of persistent prayers for her son. God was at work in his heart—on a bus in Moscow.

Reflecting on that evening, I realized that the public decisions for Christ were not the only ones that mattered. The Holy Spirit had reached Anatoly due largely to his mother's years of atomic faith in persistent prayers. The precious moments of transformation on the bus and at the public event in an atheist country were a striking reminder: God's power and work are not confined to church buildings and sermons. He is even in the simple, sincere moments, from dance floors to bus rides.

As the conversation with Anatoly deepened, I shared Scripture. "Jesus said, 'I am the way, the truth, and the life'; no one comes to the Father except through Him." Anatoly listened with his heart, evident by his barely contained emotions.

"You may not know this," I continued, "but the Bible says God didn't send His Son to condemn the world but to save it—to save you and me, . . . anyone who believes. Isn't it time to stop running from Him, Anatoly?" A tear rolled down his cheek.

"What you're feeling is something we've all felt," I affirmed. "It's the Holy Spirit tapping on your heart. This decision isn't about any specific words," I explained. "It's about trusting God with your life."

He nodded.

"Let's pray the same prayer we prayed on the dance floor, but this time, let it be personal—from your heart to God."

Several had gathered in the tight aisle, and eventually our entire team placed our hands on him, prepared to pray. His mother, too, slipped her hand onto his shoulder.

Anatoly accepted my outreached hand, and we prayed the simple, heartfelt prayer. In that sacred moment, he repented of his sins and invited Jesus into his heart and life. He made a personal decision to follow Jesus.

We embraced, and I said, "Now, Anatoly, you're in the family of God!" With a sweeping hand toward the team, I announced, "And these are your brothers and sisters. One day, we'll all be together with God in Heaven."

The evening held special significance, far more outreaching than we could know until we step into Heaven.

I learned that Anatoly's mother had faithfully prayed for him since his birth. Now, after nearly fifty years, she had witnessed her prayers answered—her son's new birth into God's family.

An overwhelming sense of gratitude and joy permeated the bus, as it had under the pavilion and through Gorky Park and into the city streets. In the unexpected turn of events, we had distributed nearly a thousand Bibles and gospel tracts to a crowd of individuals who realized their hunger to learn about Jesus. But Anatoly's transformation deeply impacted us because we'd gotten to know him and his mother and were privileged to witness her faithful prayers of fifty years answered.

After we stepped off the bus at the hotel, Anatoly approached me. Extending his hand, he clasped mine firmly. "Dale," he said with quiet sincerity, "how can I ever thank you for today? . . . Thank you." Then, without hesitation, he pulled me into an earnest embrace. More softly, he asked with wonder, "Is it true? Are we brothers now?"

I smiled warmly. "Yes, Anatoly, brothers—now, always, and forever."

Anatoly and I talked about meeting in the future, specifically me returning to Russia to speak to his students at the university. However, as life often unfolds, I haven't seen Anatoly since the day his heart and life changed. Still, I hold on to the expectation that we'll meet again, in Heaven. I believe his mother's ongoing prayers of faith were central to God placing Anatoly with our group that evening, which became the most important night of his life. That's the power of consistent prayer.

Reflecting on the Gorky Park experience reminds me that the impact of God's love is not only transformative but far-reaching. Anatoly, a man of education and worldly accomplishment, had encountered a power far more significant than his own or his government and country; he had encountered the Creator and Savior of humankind.

And in that moment of his new birth, his mother's prayers bore fruit. The doorway of Heaven had opened, and Anatoly and many others began their new life in Jesus.

Faith journeys are unique for everyone and often shaped by faithful prayers merging with unanticipated people and circumstances in unexpected places, each encounter divinely mapped by God.

How much had the prayers and fasting before the Moscow trip impacted the seemingly spontaneous revival in Gorky Park? We will not know until Heaven. However, I've noticed that when I take the time to focus in prayer and fasting, I often see God move in miraculous ways.

Fasting helps us turn our focus from our superficial lives to our relationship with God through Jesus. Hearing His voice (*rhēma*) and discerning His leadership through His Holy Spirit are paramount to experiencing a life of victory.

Why Did Jesus Teach Us To Fast?

Before Jesus began His public ministry, He fasted for forty days in the wilderness. He overcame temptation, and His reliance on His Father was strengthened. That dedicated time and those multiple experiences prepared Him for the challenges He would face throughout His mission on Earth.

Among His most familiar teachings on fasting are these: "When you fast, do not be like the hypocrites, with a sad countenance. . . . But you, when you fast, anoint your head and wash your face, so that you do not appear to men to be fasting, but to your Father" (Matthew 6:16–18).

The Heart of Effective Fasting With Prayer

Jesus emphasized fasting for His followers as a personal, humble act of faith and an expected practice with prayer. He didn't say *if* you fast but *when* you fast.

He emphasized that fasting with prayer strengthens our connection with God. Neither fasting nor praying is to gain personal attention or praise from others. Fasting is all about supercharging our private prayer life and sensitivity to God's communication with us individually.

How Does Fasting Increase the Power of Prayer?

When we set aside our physical desires and distractions to concentrate on our spiritual connection with God, our spirits become more sensitive to His Spirit within us—His inaudible promptings and His "still small voice" (1 Kings 19:12)—as demonstrated in the Moscow story. God prompted, within my heart, to seek a way to connect with the mass of people gathered in the pavilion.

Our sensitized hearts to God's *rhēma* word strengthened our power in prayer to better carry out His purposes. That increased strength also enables us to overcome the enemy's efforts to kill our prayers and actions of faith. Along with the other power tools of effective prayer (such as persistence and patience), the outcome is answered prayers.

Daniel 9:3 lists several key elements that increase the power of prayer. When he was seeking God regarding the children of Israel, captive in Babylonia, Daniel said, "I set my face [focus] toward the Lord God to make request by prayer and supplications [prayer with a spirit of reverence and devotion], with fasting [self-sacrifice], sackcloth, and ashes [humility and repentance]" (AMP, author explanations).

This Scripture gives us a powerful example of what God designed to accompany prayer and fasting: humility, repentance, and focus on a specific need.

God works through His people—not around them.

Fasting in itself does not bring answers to our prayers. In other words, fasting is not a method of twisting God's arm to get Him to respond when we pray. He is *always* speaking to us.

Fasting helps sensitize our spirits so that we can sense God's promptings. Through fasting, worldly interference is minimized, bringing us nearer to God's spiritual frequency and into closer fellowship with Him.

If you've been praying for someone or something for a long time without seeing an answer, consider adding fasting to your prayer life. Fasting can supercharge your prayers and hasten the breakthrough you're longing for.

Prolonged fasting helps your spirit rise above your fleshly desires, bringing you into closer alignment with God.

Remember, fasting doesn't change God—it changes you.

Chapter 20

YOUR PATHWAY TO PURPOSE
TRUE ELVIS PRESLEY STORIES

God, who has saved us and called us
with a holy calling, not according to
our works, but according to His own
purpose and grace which was given to us
in Christ Jesus before time began.
— 2 Timothy 1:8–9

ONCE WE UNDERSTAND THE ESSENCE OF FAITH AND GROW CONFIDENT IN APPLYING IT, FAITH CAN BECOME THE SEAMLESS UNDERLYING FOUNDATION OF OUR DAILY LIVES:

- Influencing our thoughts
- Guiding our decisions
- Shaping our actions
- Motivating our responses

According to the teachings of Jesus, when we use faith based on His unchanging Word, we're implementing His method of *supernaturally fulfilling His will.*

God created every person as an eternal being with an eternal purpose. If you are a follower of Jesus who has picked up your cross and are following Him, the next step in surrendering your will to God's is finding His unique purpose for you.

The Bible tells us in Ephesians 2:10 that we are God's handiwork, created in Christ Jesus to do good works, which God prepared in advance for us to do. The verse indicates that God has plans for everyone. And He's given us what we each need to accomplish His plans.

Every person has a specific call from God on their life. He created us with differing talents, strengths, and passions for His purposes and glory. Those gifts are not random in you; they are intentional. God has a reason for how He created you and why you are here—a purpose that no one else can fulfill in the same way *you* can.

Our uniqueness doesn't mean we're each called to do something dramatic or in the spotlight. Our purposes on this planet can take different forms in different seasons. Contrary to what most people may think, our purposes do not stop when we die. A child of God never dies in spirit. We move from life on Earth to an even more expansive life with God in Heaven throughout eternity.

What's important to remember is this: Each calling of God is invaluable to Him. Our individual purposes for existing were designed by Him for this lifetime and eternity. Every calling is vitally important to fulfilling God's will.

As we walk with Jesus, taking action by faith, listening for God's voice, and seeking His direction, we discover our unique, individual purposes.

Your lifelong mission may have unfolded in you at a young age, or you may have grown into your calling over time or by circumstances that reshaped and refined you.

You have a unique and divinely important role in God's family.

Living by faith is the backbone of discovering and following God's call. We see this demonstrated in aspects of the following real-life story. I kept this story private for over fifty years, only sharing it with family. But I believe God prompted me to share it with you now. I hope this story will encourage you as much as it has encouraged me every time it comes to mind.

A True Elvis Presley Story

About four months after my airplane crash, the captain of Elvis Presley's Lockheed JetStar invited me to take a private tour of the four-engine luxury jet, N777EP. The invitation was unexpected, and the experience was profound.

The captain had seen me in my wheelchair on the tarmac and learned about my miraculous crash survival. Perhaps his invitation was an attempt to help me reconnect with the aviation world—a world that had once been mine. At that time, no one—not doctors, family, or friends—expected me to walk again, let alone return to my long-held aviation passion, and certainly not to fly again.

During my tour aboard the Lockheed jet, the captain was interrupted and excused himself. There I sat, alone in the fuselage, in Elvis's seat.

In my heart, I felt pressed to pray for Elvis's safety in his many travels. And throughout the next thirty minutes, I experienced something truly profound. My heart started pounding so strongly that it seemed physically painful. Deep inside, I knew God's Holy Spirit was speaking to me. I sensed that Elvis was wrestling with God's call on his life—a divine calling so profound that if he fulfilled it, millions would come to know Jesus, make Him the Lord of their lives, and secure the promise of eternal life in Heaven.

But my experience in Elvis's aircraft didn't make sense to me. *Why me, God?* I wondered. *Why are You revealing this to me? And what am I to do about it?* I couldn't wrap my mind around it.

Years later, I would see in hindsight that God had been preparing me for the decades I would work as an aviation specialist. I would eventually operate from Hollywood Burbank, Van Nuys, Santa Monica, Long Beach, and various other airports across the US. In that purpose, I would become keenly aware of the numerous celebrities and high-profile musicians who had tragically lost their lives in aircraft accidents. The aviation plans God designed for me would include a passion centered on aviation safety.

From that pivotal moment on Elvis's plane in 1969, I carried a deep burden to pray fervently for his safety—Elvis Presley, the individual, the man behind the entertainer. I made it a point to pray daily for his well-being, asking God to protect him from harm and evil. I also prayed that he would be a light in the darkness, standing apart from those who might lead him astray. More importantly, I prayed that he would surrender fully to God's divine purpose for his life.

Although the experience was peculiar, I wholeheartedly embraced the Holy Spirit's message and immediately prayed for Elvis to step into his rightful place as a spiritual leader for his generation and beyond. I've prayed for many people in my lifetime, but never with such a clear, unmistakable mandate—not before or since. This was undeniably a supernatural experience.

Over time, my body continued to miraculously heal. I completed extensive aviation training and became a commercial airline pilot. From there, God led me to start my own jet aviation business and serve as a flight instructor for dozens of clients in the entertainment industry. Through that business I also fulfilled missionary work as a pilot.

Who could have predicted such a path? Only the Lord.

Here's the point: We don't know when, where, or how God will lead us to our distinctive purposes, but the pathway is paved with

- surrender to God,
- listening to His *rhēma* voice within us,
- obeying His *logos* Word, which confirms His will, and
- learning to follow Him by faith.

After decades of working as one of Hollywood's go-to experts for aviation instruction, pilot training, and aircraft management for celebrities, entertainers, and CEOs (see this book's introduction), I understood why Hollywood is often called "Tinseltown." The entire industry thrives on secrets. Truth is scarce, and perception reigns supreme, as were stories surrounding Elvis Presley.

Elvis Presley Was a Christian

Most people focused on the glamour, rumors, and wild stories surrounding Elvis, including the massive media betrayals. Few have tuned in to the truth that Elvis was a Bible-believing, Bible-carrying, Bible-reading follower of the Lord Jesus. A point of reference is a look back at his concerts. If you were to watch videos of his concerts (available online), you'd see that almost every performance featured two gospel songs in the middle of his sets.

With spiritual discernment, one can see that he delivered the gospel songs differently from his more famous hits. Elvis had a genuine, living relationship with Jesus, and when he performed those gospel songs, that spiritual relationship was evident to those who knew what to look for.

In a 2010 interview with anchor Matt Lauer, Priscilla Presley shared about Elvis's faith in Jesus. In response to what Elvis might be doing today if he were alive, she said, "I think Elvis would always be a part of music, no matter what. . . . It was in his blood. I don't know if he'd be doing rock 'n' roll right now; I think that maybe he'd be going into gospel. Maybe even preaching. . . . He loved to teach and loved the Bible."[29]

When Elvis's father remarried, his new wife came with three boys. One was Bill Stanley, who authored *The Faith of Elvis: A Story Only a Brother Can Tell.*

Before that marriage, Elvis was an only child. Gaining stepbrothers overjoyed him. Bill wrote that Elvis prayed this prayer:

> "Dear Heavenly Father, we thank You for this day and for our many blessings. Thank You for bringing these three little boys into my life. I promise to love and protect them for the rest of my life."[30]

According to Bill's book, Elvis lived out that prayer his entire life. Bill wrote that Elvis regularly read the Bible to him and his brothers and often acted out the stories. In an interview with *The Christian Post*, Bill shared, "You don't forget those Sunday school lessons."[31]

Several people I know who worked with Elvis concurred that he was a perfect gentleman—always kind, trying to please, and a listener. In short, my experience was that Elvis was a loving, sweet, and gentle man who reflected the life of Jesus Christ as he was able.

Those closest to Elvis would agree with Stanley's assessment: "Elvis didn't want to be like anyone . . . but he did want to be like Jesus."[32]

Multiple sources attribute Elvis as having said, during a concert, something to this effect: "I am not the king. Jesus Christ is the King. I'm just an entertainer."

His spiritual life is why we so often hear about the love and generosity Elvis showed to others day in and day out.

Based on my personal knowledge, I can attest that his love for people reflected his love for Jesus.

There was a time when he said, in his unmistakable Southern drawl, "Everyone is looking out for number one, . . . but Jesus said we are to surrender number one, take up our cross, and follow Him."

My experience was that any time Elvis had the opportunity, he gently but passionately lifted the name of Jesus and placed the focus on God.

During his Vegas years, Elvis encountered dire situations that are difficult to describe. He cried out to God in desperate times when pressures placed on him were illegal, unfair, and crushing. Elvis was already a believer, and Jesus was his Savior. During this crucial time, he fully surrendered, embracing Jesus not only as Savior but as the Lord of his heart and life.

What the apostle Paul said about himself was what many saw reflected in Elvis Presley, the man:

> It is no longer I who live, but Christ lives in me; and the life which I now live in the flesh I live by faith in the Son of God, who loved me and gave Himself for me. — Galatians 2:20

Here are some Bible verses that held special significance to Elvis:

> I shall not die, but live, and declare the works of the Lord. — Psalm 118:17 (KJV).

> I am crucified with Christ; nevertheless I liveth; yet not I, but Christ liveth in me. — Galatians 2:20 (KJV)

> If anyone is in Christ, he is a new creation; old things
> have passed away; behold, all things have become
> new. — 2 Corinthians 5:17

You may be surprised to learn that I never attended an Elvis concert or visited Graceland. It's not that I didn't enjoy his music—I did. And I would have enjoyed going to a concert or touring Graceland and the museum in Memphis. It's just that those things were not a priority for me. My interest was in the man behind the entertainer, the one who God loved and who I believed was chosen for a special calling. My assignment from the Lord was straightforward: Pray with unwavering faith for Elvis Presley, trusting that God's perfect will would be fulfilled in his life. I continued to pray for him after that experience.

Did Elvis fulfill his calling according to the prophetic message I received aboard his jet in 1969? I assure you, with absolute certainty, the answer is a resounding yes. He fulfilled God's call and exceeded every expectation that we who knew and loved him could have imagined.

If Elvis were here today and a guest on my podcast, I'd ask him, "What's the most important thing you'd say to anyone listening to this podcast?" (Visit DaleBlack.org.)

I'm certain Elvis's reply would be something like this: "Learn about Jesus. Read about His life and read His teachings. Learn what He taught. You don't need to follow a religion, a denomination, or a preacher to get to Heaven. Turn to Jesus and ask Him to forgive your sins. Ask Him to come into your heart and take over your life. Pick up your cross and follow Jesus, and He will bless you. Heaven will be your home, and you'll be forever glad you put your faith in Him."

Finding God's purpose makes life—even in the tough times—feel meaningful and worthwhile. Discovering your God-given purpose brings joy, passion, and deep contentment.

I agree with Priscilla when she said, "If Elvis were alive today, music would always be a part of his life because it's in his blood."

Frankly, I imagine Elvis would sing and lead others in a variety of songs as long as they pointed people to God and glorified the name of Jesus. And I don't think anything could have kept Elvis from preaching the gospel of Jesus to any who would listen. He loved the Bible because he loved the Lord, and he preached because he had a deep love for God and His people.

Looking back on my own prompting to pray for Elvis, I trust that God had a plan and a reason for tapping me in while I was sitting in Elvis's jet. I believe our prayers ripple through eternity, continuing until they fulfill God's divine purpose. In that truth, I am humbled and find joy and peace.

God's Call Requires Faith

Finding and following God's call on our lives requires what this book is dedicated to explaining: faith—specifically supernatural faith, biblical faith, what I also call *atomic faith*.

As you've seen throughout this book—and certainly in the Word of God—belief is the fuel of faith. The igniting of our belief gives us the courage and trust to step into God's callings with atomic faith and receive what He has planned for us.

Belief is the fuel of faith and helps us believe in the unseen.

Often God's plan isn't immediately clear. Faith is what bridges the gap to clarity. Let's revisit faith's meaning from Hebrews 11:1: Faith is confidence in what we hope for and assurance about what we do not yet see.

Faith enables us to move forward even when we're unsure of the details. Faith is trusting that God will reveal each step and detail along the way as it is needed.

A walk of faith gives us the courage to face obstacles.

We will continue to face challenges, doubts, mistakes, and even moments of temporary failure. Think of biblical figures such as Moses and David. They had callings from God, yet each faced intense struggles and failures. What kept them pressing through was their faith in God's character and His promises. They trusted God to provide them with courage, guidance, strength to overcome obstacles, and all else they needed to succeed. And God did! He is faithful.

Faith is a powerful tool that demonstrates through our actions our belief that *God is with us* (Matthew 28:20) and

God is for us (Romans 8:31), no matter how difficult the calling or the journey.

Faith helps us trust God's timing.

We may feel ready for big things immediately, but God often leads us through seasons of preparation first. Just because we sense a calling doesn't mean every door will suddenly open. Faith requires our patience and believing without a doubt that God's timing is always perfect. Our prayers and standing in faith reveal what we truly believe in our hearts.

Reflecting on my life, I often thought I was waiting on God when, in reality, God was waiting on me!

Faith is like a muscle; it needs exercise to become stronger.

A walk of faith strengthens us to surrender our fears and doubts and grow confident in the integrity of God and His Word.

There will be times when following God's call feels too risky or too challenging. You may feel inadequate or fear that you'll fail. But living by faith will encourage you to hold fast to your knowledge of the truth (2 Timothy 1:13).

God's power is greater than our weaknesses.

When Jesus stood on the Sea of Galilee and called Peter to step out of the boat and walk to Him on the water (Matthew 14:29), Peter's faith got him moving. The verse tells us that Peter walked on the water—until the moment his focus shifted to the waves, the natural circumstances around him.

Taking his eyes off Jesus rather than holding his gaze and continuing in firm faith, he moved into fear and doubt and began to sink. But Jesus was there and lifted him up to safety.

Faith isn't being unafraid. Faith is choosing to trust God with faith over fear.

A Life Without Purpose

I've watched many people retire in their later years. After decades of hard work, retirement feels like the ultimate goal—the moment of crossing the finish line. I see retirement differently now. After watching my father and father-in-law retire, I realized how quickly retirement can take a toll.

Nowhere in the Bible do I see retirement. What I see is a shift—a slowing down to share wisdom, guiding others, and to draw closer to the Lord, growing deeper in relationship with Him and His Word.

God's path is passion, purpose, and true joy, with peace in knowing who you are in His Kingdom. Such joy requires surrendering our own plans and embracing God's purpose with faith, even at the cost of our own desires. As Jesus reminds us in Matthew 10:39,

"He who finds his life will lose it, and he who loses his life for My sake will find it."

This life of purpose with contentment comes only from living in agreement with God's will.

Perhaps you've been feeling that life isn't worth the struggle. Maybe your passion faded long ago, and hope feels distant. There is great news: God has a unique purpose for you, regardless of your age, stage, or status in life. You can find His purpose—it is awaiting you!—and you can fulfill it and once again be driven with passion and fulfillment.

While you may not uncover your purpose overnight, you can trust in God's promises that He *will* lead you step by step when you earnestly seek Him. Ask in faith for Him to reveal the unique role He has designed for you. Life can begin anew at any age and any crossroad in life. His plans for you never end.

As the Lord declares in His Word,

> "I know the thoughts that I think toward you, . . . thoughts of peace and not of evil, to give you a future and a hope." — Jeremiah 29:11

Trust in His promise.

No matter where life has taken you—into detours, disappointments, or even despair—God is not finished with you. His purpose for your life remains firmly rooted in you, waiting to be discovered.

When you align your heart with His, you will find not only your calling but also a joy beyond words. Your passion will reignite, your hope will be restored, and you will walk forward with confidence, knowing that your life is unfolding exactly as God intended.

Jesus said, "With God nothing will be impossible." Exercise atomic faith in His promises, and you will discover that your best is yet to come.

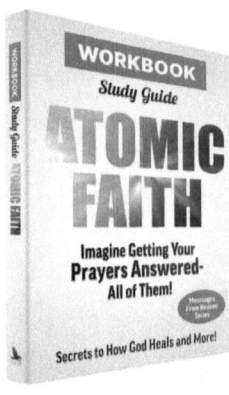

Chapter 21

SECRETS TO GETTING
RESULTS THAT LAST

"And I will give you the keys of the kingdom
of heaven, and whatever you bind on earth
will be bound in heaven, and whatever you
loose on earth will be loosed in heaven."
— Matthew 16:19

FROM HEAVEN'S PERSPECTIVE, THIS FINAL CHAPTER IS JUST THE BEGINNING OF YOUR PERSONAL JOURNEY OF LIVING BY FAITH. You've been introduced to that most powerful way to live—the lifestyle of atomic faith that aligns with God's will and His ways.

Throughout this book, we've explored real-life stories of people who overcame incredible challenges through faith in God. My hope and prayer are that those examples have not only inspired you but deeply stirred a desire to experience that kind of powerful, personal relationship with Jesus—where prayers aren't just heard but answered.

You've gained new insight into what faith is and how it works. You've seen that the miracles in the Bible are also the miracles happening today as a result of faith in action. You've seen that faith isn't just a concept . . . it's an active response to what you believe in your heart.

Faith is an active response to what you believe in your heart.

We've also examined the difference between natural faith and supernatural (atomic) faith. Natural faith helps to make what's already possible more likely. And while natural faith can produce incredible outcomes, its power is limited.

Supernatural faith, as we've seen, makes the seemingly impossible a reality. Atomic faith is the faith we see in the Bible—the faith Jesus taught His disciples. With supernatural (atomic) faith, there are no earthly limits.

We've discussed the three keys to getting your prayers answered:

- **Hope** is looking forward with expectation.
- **Belief** is trusting that something is true.
- **Faith** is acting on what you believe.

According to Scripture, your faith is how God provides the answers you need.

- Faith begins with hope, which grows into belief.
- As belief strengthens, it becomes deeply rooted in your heart.
- When you act on what you believe, the unseen becomes visible.

A single act of faith, repeated over time, leads to transformation.

Imagine a farmer planting just one seed. He wouldn't expect a great harvest from only a single seed, would he? Even planting twenty seeds wouldn't make for a prosperous farm. But what if he plants another twenty? And another, and another, . . . ? Over time, his farm thrives because he consistently and persistently sowed seeds.

We've seen that faith works in the same way. Can a single act of faith change your life? Yes, it can. But *lasting transformation* comes from repeatedly stepping out in faith in response to every challenge—building your faith muscle.

What if you were to take one step of faith, then another, and another? Eventually, you'd look back and see that your day-to-day life has entirely transformed—all due to that first small step of faith.

When you consistently apply hope, belief, and faith—building one answered prayer upon another—you're stepping into the "abundant life" Jesus promised in John 10:10. That is my hope for you.

Living by faith is a lifelong journey of consistent persistence that has no finish line. Instead of a finish line, think of your new life in Jesus as an exciting adventure in which you're constantly growing and improving, right up to your last earthly breath.

Yes, you'll need faith to overcome the challenges of this fallen world, but remember, atomic faith is not faith in yourself or in the idea of faith.

Atomic faith is faith in God and His promises.

Imagine the incredible impact of applying supernatural faith every day in every circumstance throughout the day.

- Think about what you could accomplish in your business if you refused to quit.
- Picture the strength you could maintain if you kept training without giving up.
- Imagine how healthy you could become if you stayed committed to nutritious eating, continued learning about wellness, and never gave up on yourself.
- Think of the knowledge you could gain if you never stopped learning.
- Imagine the legacy you could leave by discovering God's purpose for your life and living in the center of His will.
- Consider the deep, meaningful friendships you could build if you never stopped giving and caring for others.

Small acts of faith don't just add up—they *compound*. And because they connect you to God's power, they don't just grow—they *multiply*.

That's the power of atomic faith.

Now imagine having your prayers answered—yes, *all of them*.

Fasten Your Seatbelt

If you're choosing to live by faith—atomic faith—fasten your seatbelt! You're in for an adventurous life filled with great blessings and victories. But be prepared for a bumpy ride: Life is loaded with tribulation. You will be wrestling against satan, his demons, and the godlessness of this fallen world. But Jesus said that those who believe in Him have been given His power, with which you *are* able to overcome every obstacle.

Thankfully, as a believer in Jesus Christ, you have the superior power tools and weapons to overcome any and every evil that comes your way. By committing to following Jesus and His teachings, *nothing* is too difficult for you! Defeat will no longer be an option.

Also, when you use atomic faith correctly, answers to your prayers will arrive more quickly and effectively than you've previously experienced! And unanswered prayers will be a thing of the past!

Flying With Faith

Great job, my friend. You've completed Faith's "Before Takeoff" checklist!

- ✓ You've read the truths of God's Word, referenced throughout this book.
- ✓ You now understand that atomic faith is the missing link between God's power and your prayers being answered.
- ✓ You've learned what faith is and what faith is not.
- ✓ You've learned how to walk by faith, not by sight.
- ✓ You've learned how use the power tools of faith that bring God's will to Earth as it is in Heaven.

By applying *hope, belief,* and *faith* in God and His promises, you'll rise above and overcome the difficulties and obstacles that once held you back. You can do it! I'm on the sidelines praying for you and cheering you on.

And you'll hear from me again. If not in the next book, you'll see me smiling when we greet each other at our heavenly destination.

Well done, my friend. Lift your mind, heart, and life toward Heaven. Miracles are waiting, but they won't automatically meet you on Earth's runway; you've got to take off and fly by using your faith. Then you'll rise above the clouds and turbulence, into the clear skies of God's promises.

Now it's your turn. The controls are in your hands. Engage your faith, throttle forward, and takeoff. Trust the wind that God provides—and soar like the eagle you were born to be.

BEFORE YOU GO . . .

A COMPLIMENTARY GIFT

First, thank you for joining me on this journey through *Atomic Faith*. It has been my honor and privilege to share God's powerful faith principles and true stories of atomic faith with you.

If you're inspired by *Atomic Faith*, you may also enjoy our other books, described in the following pages.

In addition, I have a gift for you:

Get your

***Powerful Scripture
Promises to Fuel
Your Faith***
at
DaleBlack.org.

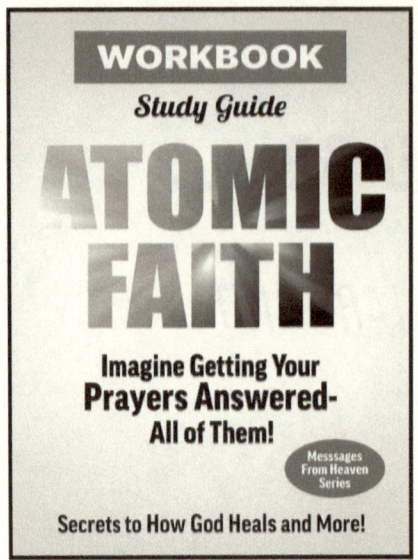

You've just finished reading Atomic Faith and are ready to act on the powerful, life-changing truths that can lead to the prayer breakthrough you've longed for. Whether studying with a small group or alone, this workbook is for you! Possibly, you've read *Atomic Faith* but need a refresher on what faith is, how it's designed to work, how God heals, and the secrets to releasing Heaven's power. This study guide, designed specifically to get the most out of Capt. Dale Black's teachings in *Atomic Faith*, serves as a standalone and as an ideal companion to the book. Start improving your life today and step into the abundant lifestyle Jesus designed for you.

ATOMIC FAITH
STUDY GUIDE

*Over 101 activities to taking effective action

*Chapter summaries with key takeaways

*Faith principles with practical suggestions

*Easy to follow ideas to get results

*And MUCH more!

Capt. Dale Black is a seasoned expert in living by faith, partnering with God to make the impossible possible. As the only survivor of a plane crash, Dale was given no hope of living a normal life. From a coma with life-threatening injuries to being confined to a wheelchair with no hope of walking, seeing, or recovering his memory, he found the  hidden principles that make the power of faith work. Dale became a dedicated student of the Bible, delving into the miracle-working power of Jesus. This journey led him to uncover what he calls the "secrets of atomic faith."

DaleBlack.org

Riveting! Shocking! Eye-Opening!

HOW I BEAT TERMINAL CANCER
Using SPIRITUAL TRUTHS and the NATURAL LAWS of Health

Life,
Cancer
and
God

HEALING YOUR
BODY, SOUL & SPIRIT

Paula Black *and* Capt. Dale Black, PhD

Statistics state that 1 in 2 men and 1 in 3 women will get cancer in their lifetime. Reading this book could save your life. — **Rhonda McCue,** RN and Hospice Nurse

FORGET EVERYTHING YOU THOUGHT YOU KNEW ABOUT CANCER! The author's approach is startling—the "missing link" for those dealing with cancer. Everyone should read this book! — **Dr. Robert W. Christensen,** Maxillofacial Surgeon and Author

If someone you love is dealing with cancer, you owe it to your family to read this book! — **Kara Black**

A compelling story of healing. Now Paula and Dale help others survive and thrive. It worked for Paula, for scores of others. It can work for you. — **William E. Knopp,** Sr. Pastor, First Baptist Church

Life, Cancer and God is the essential guide to beating cancer.

In the prime of life, Paula heard the dreaded words, "It's cancer." Doctors gave her three to six months to live. She met with doctors and oncologists and spoke with cancer patients—while tirelessly researching every conventional and alternative cancer treatment available. Twenty months after diagnosis, her advanced-stage cancer was gone, without chemotherapy or radiation. That was over twenty-five years ago.

The author's journey from advanced-stage cancer to near-death to complete health is a faith-based BEST SELLER.

PaulaBlack.org

A Plane Crash … A Lone Survivor …
A Journey to Heaven and Back

Of all the books about Heaven, this one's the best! — **Tim Breuninger,** San Diego, CA

Next to the Bible, Flight To Heaven *is the BEST BOOK I have ever read!* — **Pastor Shawn Machen,** Sr. Pastor, World Victory Church, Moody, AL

One of the most inspiring books I have ever read! — **Mike Biden**, Retired SAR Pilot

Wow! This story has edified my faith that God is who He says He is and will do what He said He will do!! — **Debbie Newman,** Memphis, TN

I could not put this book down, and I cried through much of it. Flight To Heaven *is the most moving and inspirational book I have ever read.* — **Donna Benton,** New York, NY

A beautifully written and amazing account of life, death—and life again. In the early days of his flying career, Capt. Dale Black was a passenger in a horrific airplane crash, which some have called the most ironic in aviation history. He was the only survivor. In the gruesome aftermath, Dale experienced a life-changing journey to Heaven. Not only was Dale's life forever altered, but his story has changed the lives of millions. This story is full of challenges and struggles that culminate in atomic faith, guaranteed to inspire. Dale's flight to heaven dramatically changed his life. Reading this book could change yours!

DaleBlack.org

Miracles . . . Followed by the Miraculous!

Driven by ambition, Dale Black's entire life was fixated on personal success . . . until the day everything changed.

As the only survivor of a horrific plane crash, he encountered the spectacular glories of Heaven. After waking from a three-day coma, Dale made a supernatural physical recovery, and against all odds, he fulfilled his dream of becoming an airline pilot instructor.

CAPT. DALE BLACK flew for forty years as a professional pilot, but one flight transformed him forever—a journey to Heaven!

Here's what readers are saying:

Lessons for Life and Leaning More About Heaven

This book blew me away. As a nurse, I've heard from patients who were brought back from death, but nothing has ever come close to Dale's description. This book has deepened my faith and caused me to seek a deeper relationship with God. — **Nurse Rhonda**

Best Description of Heaven EVER!

Everyone needs this book. I would buy this book as a gift in a heartbeat. — **Lorraine R.**

Retired 747 Captain Gives 5 Stars

I bought this as a gift for my husband, a retired 747 captain. He loved this book so much, he ordered three other books by Dale Black! He has always been a man who loved the Lord, but this book renewed his faith in a way I've seen nothing else do. He now truly has a RELATIONSHIP with Jesus. — **Lisa K.**

DaleBlack.org

Will I Go to Heaven?

Have you ever stopped to ask yourself, *Am I 100 percent sure I'll go to Heaven when I die?*

It's a big question that can make us pause and think about our beliefs regarding life after death. Many of us have doubts or unanswered questions . . . and that's completely normal.

If you're not certain about your eternal destination, I invite you to visit a page on my website as noted below. There, you'll find ideas and discussions that may help you explore what the Bible says about how to get to Heaven when your life on Earth ends. And perhaps you'll also gain a clearer understanding of what awaits believers beyond this life.

Visit ***BOOK YOUR HEAVEN FLIGHT***

at **DaleBlack.org**

Messages from Heaven Series

God has placed a powerful calling on my heart: to write the *Messages from Heaven Series*, sharing decades of walking by faith.

The first book in the series, *Atomic Faith*, is just the beginning. More books are in progress— exploring vital topics like Prophetic End Times, How God Heals, Modern Miracles, Demons: Your Invisible Enemy, Power in Prayer, the Holy Spirit, and many MORE!

But we need your help to bring them to life.

Traditional publishers often silence the truth. So I've been led by the Lord to self-publish. No compromising. I'm relying on the support of readers like you to help.

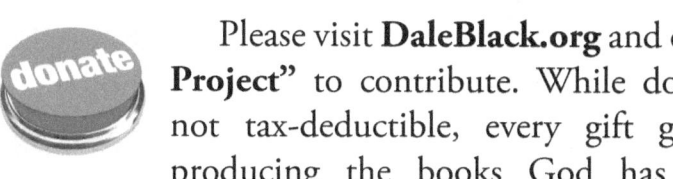

Please visit **DaleBlack.org** and click **"Book Project"** to contribute. While donations are not tax-deductible, every gift goes toward producing the books God has called me to write and publish. Together, let's keep this mission moving forward.

Support the book series at DaleBlack.org.
Thank you.

Follow Dale Black

DaleBlack.org

Follow Paula Black

PaulaBlack.org

When Someone You Know Has Cancer...

Check out

Paula's Cancer Coaching Program
PaulaBlack.org

ENDNOTES

1. *Merriam-Webster*, s.v. "atomic (*adj.*)," accessed March 28, 2025, https://www.merriam-webster.com/dictionary/atom.

2. *Cambridge Dictionary*, s.v. "atomic (*adj.*)," accessed March 23, 2025, https://dictionary.cambridge.org/dictionary/english/atomic.

3. Hebrews 11:1.

4. Hebrews 11:1.

5. "Amelia Earhart – Aviator, Trendsetter, Legacy," Amelia Earhart Hangar Museum, accessed March 1, 2022, https://ameliaearharthangarmuseum.org/amelia-earhart/.

6. *Merriam-Webster*, s.v. "hope (*n.*)," accessed September 11, 2024, https://www.merriam-webster.com/dictionary/hope.

7. *Merriam-Webster*, s.v. "hope (*n.*)."

8. Johnny Cash, "Guideposts Classics: Johnny Cash on Overcoming Addiction," *Guideposts*, accessed August 3, 2022, https://guideposts.org/positive-living/health-and-wellness/addiction-and-recovery/guideposts-classics-johnny-cash-on-overcoming-addiction/.

9. Sports Spectrum Media, "RIP George Foreman," March 24, 2025, https://youtube.com/shorts/jc38CU5QMqI?si=y2hwSmzwSM6PfA_R.

10. Craig Scott, "Exclusive: George Foreman – 'a Man; a Fighter . . . ,'" Features, Boxing Social, April 12, 2020, https://boxing-social.com/features/exclusive-george-foreman-man-fighter/.

11. Dave Zirin, "An Interview with George Foreman," CounterPunch.org, November 7, 2003, https://www .counterpunch.org/2003/11/07/an-interview-with-george-foreman/.

12. William Gildea, "Seeking to Understand George Foreman," *Los Angeles Times*, January 14, 1990, https://www.latimes.com/ archives/la-xpm-1990-01-14-sp-455-story.html.

13. George Foreman and Ken Abraham, *God In My Corner: A Spiritual Memoir* (Thomas Nelson, 2007), 26–27.

14. Foreman and Abraham, *God In My Corner*, 27.

15. Michael Foust, "'I Found Jesus': George Foreman Says 1977 near-Death Experience Changed His Life," Crosswalk.com, last updated April 13, 2023, https://www.crosswalk.com/headlines/ contributors/michael-foust/i-found-jesus-george-foreman-says-1977-near-death-experience-changed-his-life.html.

16. Australian Prayer Network, "Boxer George Foreman Recalls Incredible Conversion to Faith in God," Australian Prayer Network, June 18, 2023, https://ausprayernet.org .au/2023/06/18/boxer-george-foreman-recalls-incredible-conversion-to-faith-in-god/.

17. Cooper Dowd, "George Foreman Recalls Near Death Experience: 'There Is a Living God,'" Movieguide, April 13, 2023, https://www.movieguide.org/news-articles/george-foreman-recalls-near-death-experience-there-is-a-living-god .html.

18. Foreman and Abraham, *God In My Corner*, 99.

19. George Foreman and James Lund, *Going the Extra Smile: Discovering the Life-Changing Power of a Positive Outlook* (Thomas Nelson, 2007), 17.

20. Foreman and Abraham, *God In My Corner*, 166.

21. Foreman and Abraham, *God In My Corner*, 102.

22. Foreman and Abraham, *God In My Corner*, 161.

23. Foreman and Abraham, *God In My Corner*, 98.

24. Dowd, "George Foreman Recalls Near Death Experience."

25. *Strong's Exhaustive Concordance of the Bible*, Greek Lexicon, s.v. "4102. πίστις (pistis) – faith, belief, trust, confidence, fidelity," accessed January 17, 2025, https://biblehub.com/greek/4102 .htm.

26. *Strong's Exhaustive Concordance of the Bible*, Greek Lexicon, s.v. "4100. πιστεύω (pisteuó) – to believe, to have faith, to trust," accessed January 17, 2025, https://biblehub.com/greek/4100 .htm.

27. *Strong's Exhaustive Concordance of the Bible*, Greek Lexicon, s.v. "1249. διάκονος (diakonos) – servant, minister, deacon," accessed January 17, 2025, https://biblehub.com/greek/1249 .htm.

28. *Merriam-Webster*, s.v. "persistence (*n.*)," accessed January 18, 2025, https://www.merriam-webster.com/dictionary/ persistence.

29. Mike Celizic, "Priscilla Presley: Elvis Would Be Preaching Now," Pop Culture, TODAY.com, January 8, 2010, https:// www.today.com/popculture/priscilla-presley-elvis-would-be- preaching-now-wbna34765087.

30. Billy Stanley and Kent Sanders, *The Faith of Elvis: A Story Only a Brother Can Tell* (Nelson Books, 2022), 9.

31. Jeannie Ortega Law, "'Elvis Wanted to Be like Jesus, Read His Bible Every Day,' Stepbrother Says," *The Christian Post*, October 6, 2022, https://www.christianpost.com/books/elvis-wanted-to- be-like-jesus-stepbrother-says.html.

32. Law, "'Elvis Wanted to Be like Jesus.'"

MORE PRAISES FOR
ATOMIC FAITH

Lou Peterson, leader, Living Faith Men's Ministry
When a man finds himself in the presence of the Lord, he receives a unique insight. Dale Black has taken that insight and masterfully woven the Word of God with powerful stories of faithfulness, making *Atomic Faith* both inspiring and accessible to every reader.

Lorraine Rogers, teacher and minister, Calvary Chapel School – Costa Mesa, CA
Atomic Faith shows there's nothing too hard for God! Dale Black doesn't just talk about faith—he lives it. He explains the difference between hoping and truly believing then acting on that belief. I've known Dale since childhood, and after visiting him in the hospital following the 1969 crash, I've watched God move powerfully in his life. From his stellar books *Flight to Heaven* to *Life, Cancer and God* to *Visiting Heaven*, Dale's teaching and real-life stories are unforgettable—and *Atomic Faith* is the powerful next chapter.

Ron Benson, Captain, US Air Force (retired)

Atomic Faith is a must-read for anyone looking to grow stronger in their faith journey. It's both inspirational and thought-provoking—filled with real-life insights that challenge and encourage us to trust God more deeply.

Terry Kelly, Captain, Boeing 747, United Airlines (retired)

I've read all of Dale's books—but this one is his best yet. *Atomic Faith* shows every reader how to activate God's power and get prayers answered. Through intense trials and the testing of his faith after the airplane crash, Dale discovered firsthand that with God, all things are possible. God healed him, restored him, and opened doors he never imagined. This book is powerful, practical, and truly inspiring!

Ronald J. Short, heavy equipment operator / instructor / mechanic / welder

This isn't just a book—*Atomic Faith* is a treasure. It lifted my spirit, touched my heart, and strengthened my faith. Oh, if only everyone could read this book!

Dodie Ulrich, prayer intercessor for Dale and Paula Black since 1981

Capt. Dale Black has always displayed a genuine, abiding love for God and His Word. *Atomic Faith* is a powerful result of that love—and of Dale's deep desire to see others saved, healed, and restored. After reading just a few chapters, my heart was stirred and my faith took a giant leap! Through the many life experiences he shares, Dale provides a clear path to understanding what faith truly is—along with practical ways to activate it and see your prayers answered.

Carlo Lucido, senior account executive, Home Depot (retired)

Meeting Capt. Dale Black in person changed my life—transforming me from a taker into a servant. Reading *Atomic Faith* didn't just confirm those convictions; it inspired me to serve at an even deeper level and push the limits of what it means to live by faith.

Gerry Bierly, high school teacher (retired)

Atomic Faith is a powerful reflection of the journey I saw unfold in real-time. I played college baseball with Dale and knew him before and after the crash. I witnessed his amazing recovery firsthand. This book truly knocks it out of the park, blending Dale's passion for the Lord with his love for aviation. A must-read for both new believers and seasoned Christians alike!

Jacques LaFrance, author, *Heaven Is Beyond Imagination*

I highly recommend anything Dale Black writes—especially *Atomic Faith*. In this powerful book, Dale shares faith-building experiences that help readers understand how real faith works in everyday life. He teaches that God is both faithful and capable—and that miracles often come when we trust without wavering, even at the last minute. *Atomic Faith* will show you how to walk in that kind of unwavering, transformational faith. It's rooted in Scripture and filled with real-life examples. This book is a true gift.

www.ingramcontent.com/pod-product-compliance
Lightning Source LLC
Chambersburg PA
CBHW021608120626
46545CB00001B/127